j 372.3
V36s

Seeds, Flowers, and Trees

SO-AET-206

DETROIT PUBLIC LIBRARY
WILDER BRANCH LIBRARY
7140 E. SEVEN MILE RD.
DETROIT, MI 48234

DATE DUE

BC-3

SEP '96

WI

Other Books by Barbara Dondiego

After School Crafts

Crafts for Kids: A Month-by-Month Idea Book, 2nd edition

Year-Round Crafts for Kids

Other Books in this Series by Barbara Dondiego and Rhonda Vansant

Cats, Dogs, and Classroom Pets: Science in Art, Song, and Play

Moths, Butterflies, Other Insects, and Spiders: Science in Art, Song, and Play

Shells, Whales, and Fish Tails: Science in Art, Song, and Play

About the Authors

Barbara Dondiego holds a master degree in education from the University of Virginia and a bachelor of science degree in foods and nutrition from Oregon State University. She is a state-certified educational consultant who conducts regular workshops for preschool teachers.

Rhonda Vansant has a doctorate in education from Vanderbilt University, has taught classes at both elementary and college levels, and serves as an educational consultant. She conducts workshops and gives conference presentations on methodologies for teaching young children. Rhonda is also a member of the National Association for the Education of Young Children and the Association of Childhood Education International.

About the Illustrator

Claire Kalish holds a bachelor of arts degree from Adelphi University. A former teacher, she is the owner of an Atlanta business, Table Fables.

Seeds, Flowers, and Trees
Science in Art, Song, and Play

Rhonda Vansant, Ed.D.

Barbara L. Dondiego, M.Ed.

Illustrations by

Claire Kalish

Science in Every Sense

**LEARNING
TRIANGLE
PRESS**

*Connecting
kids, parents, and teachers
through learning*

An imprint of McGraw-Hill
New York San Francisco Washington, D.C. Auckland Bogotá Caracas
Lisbon London Madrid Mexico City Milan Montreal New Delhi
San Juan Singapore Sydney Tokyo Toronto

McGraw-Hill

*A Division of The **McGraw·Hill** Companies*

©1996 by The McGraw-Hill Companies, Inc.

Printed in the United States of America. All rights reserved. The publisher takes no responsibility for the use of any materials or methods described in this book, nor for the products thereof.

Except as expressly provided in this paragraph, no part of this book may be reproduced or distributed in any form or by any means, or stored in a database or retrieval system, without the prior written permission of the publisher. Permission is granted for the original purchaser to make photocopies of the material for individual or classroom use, except that purchase of this book does not allow reproduction for an entire school or school district. Under no circumstances will any reproduction of the material be either sold or distributed on a commercial basis.

This book is printed on recycled paper containing a minimum of 50% total recycled fiber with 15% postconsumer de-inked fiber.

pbk   1 2 3 4 5 6 7 8 9 BBC/BBC 9 0 0 9 8 7 6

Product or brand names used in this book may be trade names or trademarks. Where we believe that there may be proprietary claims to such trade names or trademarks, the name has been used with an initial capital or it has been capitalized in the style used by the name claimant. Regardless of the capitalization used, all such names have been used in an editorial manner without any intent to convey endorsement of or other affiliation with the name claimant. Neither the author nor the publisher intends to express any judgment as to the validity or legal status of any such proprietary claims.

ISBN 0-07-017909-3

McGraw-Hill books are available at special quantity discounts to use as premiums and sales promotions, or for use in corporate training programs. For more information, please write to the Director of Special Sales, McGraw-Hill, 11 West 19th Street, New York, NY 10011. Or contact your local bookstore.

Acquisitions editor: Judith Terrill-Breuer
Editorial team: David M. McCandless, Associate Managing/Book Editor
        Lori Flaherty, Executive Editor
        Jennifer M. Secula, Indexer
Production team: Katherine G. Brown, Director
        Ollie Harmon, Coding
        Wanda S. Ditch, Desktop Operator
        Lorie L. White, Proofreading
        Janice Ridenour, Computer Artist
Design team: Jaclyn J. Boone, Designer
        Katherine Lukaszewicz, Associate Designer   0179093
                                                                 SIES

To my husband's parents, my dear in-laws, who grow apples, flowers, vegetables, and many other treasures of nature, which they graciously share with their family and friends.

With love,
Rhonda

To my talented daughter, Elizabeth, who adds so much to my books.

With loving thanks,
Mom

Acknowledgments

We would like to thank Pike Nursery in Marietta, Georgia, for allowing us to use their nursery for photographing the cover of this book. We would like to thank Joseph Holzman and Chantel Hayward for being in the cover photograph. We appreciate the artwork contributed by Elizabeth Dondiego, who designed the covers of the three cookbooks, and Joanna Vansant, who drew the Wildlife Tree.

Contents

A Letter to Teachers   *viii*

A Letter to Parents   *ix*

Introduction   *x*

1 Seeds   *1*

2 Flowers   *41*

3 Trees   *69*

Index   *115*

A Letter to Teachers

Dear Teacher,

You might be one of many educators who feels a certain anxiety about teaching science. Perhaps your science courses in school and college were stressful as you plodded through specific experiments, tried to memorize the periodic table, and tried to understand phenomena without the opportunity to build concepts first. You probably have forgotten much of the science instruction because it went only into short-term memory and had no direct link to what you were encountering in your world at that time. Perhaps you never had a role model who felt a passion about loving and caring for the world—a role model who would dare to teach you "how" to learn rather than "what" to learn. Whether you place yourself in this category or were blessed with good role models who instilled in you a zeal for learning science, we hope this book will contribute to meaningful and enjoyable science instruction in your class.

Because we embrace the definition that science for young children is studying and exploring our world, we strongly feel that science should be the focus of an Early Childhood curriculum. Although this is a science book, it is also a book about life and learning. It is designed to serve as a framework for a thematic study. We have provided many teaching and learning activities that involve varied content areas. Within this framework, you can also creatively add your own literature, math experiences, writing experiences, and other activities that meet the specific needs of your children. The format of this book allows your teaching and learning experiences to flow naturally together in an integrated way.

The time that it takes to complete the varied activities depends upon the age of the children and the number of children involved. The time involved is also affected by the ways you integrate the learning activities in this book with other aspects of the curriculum.

We hope that you will find this to be a comfortable format for teaching science and that you will enjoy, with your students, the journey of discovery. Perhaps you will be one who will inspire this generation of children to find joy and excitement in learning about the wonders that surround us.

Sincerely,

Rhonda Vansant

Barbara L. Dowling

A Letter to Parents

Dear Parents,

Generations of children have grown up feeling that science was too difficult, too stressful. Many children have avoided science and ranked it among their least favorite subjects.

How wonderful to think that we might change that attitude for the current generation. We, the authors, view science as studying and exploring our world in ways that are appropriate for the learner's stage of development. Children explore the world quite naturally, and we want to build upon the natural inclinations of children by guiding their explorations and nurturing their curiosity. When children see their ice cream melt, they have an opportunity to learn about their world. When children feel the wind blow, they are discovering information about their world. We do not have to search for expensive equipment to teach science to young children; we simply need to take advantage of everything that is already around us.

One of the most precious gifts we can give our children is a love of learning. We hope you will find ways to use this book with your own children as well as with groups of children in various organizations. It is our hope that you will nurture your children's natural wonder and curiosity about our world and that the dream that this generation will come to love, understand, and cherish this world will come true.

Sincerely,

Rhonda Vansant

Barbara L. Dondiego

Introduction

Seeds, flowers, and trees are essential components of our life support system on earth. Children experience these forms of nature almost every day, and it is vitally important that children grow up with an understanding and deep appreciation for them. Because seeds, flowers, and trees are readily accessible to us, they are perfect topics for scientific study. Most importantly, such a study will help children develop a respect for all living things and, hopefully, a desire to take better care of our world.

Building concepts

Studying plants allows children to experience real objects or living things, something called a *concrete experience*. If the topic of study is trees, for example, we should provide children with opportunities to investigate real trees. When we do so, we are *building a concept*. Concepts are the foundation for subsequent learning. After children experience reality, they can then make models or recreate the experience in a variety of ways. Models and pictures are called *semi-concrete representations*. Words that we attach to these experiences and representations are called *symbolic representations*. The word *tree* written in a book symbolizes a living thing for which we now have a concept. Giving children opportunities to experience real living and nonliving things helps them develop concepts that, in turn, give meaning to the written and spoken word.

Seeds, Flowers, and Trees provides guidance for helping children build concepts and then use these concepts as a foundation for a multitude of learning activities. The book is written as a cross-curricular guide to enable teachers and parents to teach children about these topics all day long if desired. Each topic of study includes the following:

☐ *Art*: Creating lifelike models

☐ *Creative drama*: Acting, pretending

☐ *Music and dancing*: Singing songs and moving creatively

☐ *Informational books*: Finding facts

☐ *Research*: Using the five senses to discover information; reading and looking at pictures; talking to people

☐ *Writing*: Preparing factual reports or creating essays, poems, or stories to express thoughts and emotions

☐ *Cooking*: Using a variety of skills to create treats

☐ *Mathematics*: Measuring, counting

Each chapter in this book presents factual information you can read aloud to the children. You might want the children to sit on the floor near you while you share this information. If you keep a chart of important words for the children's future writing, place it nearby so that you can add words throughout your reading and discussion time.

Teaching children science

For young children, science should not be a set of experiments with specific steps to be followed. Instead, it should involve a very natural discovery of their world through real experiences, creative art, literature, drama, music, writing, reading, and play. Whenever we teach children to use their five senses, we are teaching science. Whenever we provide opportunities for exploration and discovery, we are teaching science. Whenever we help children get to know the world around them, we are teaching science. Whenever we teach children to love and care for the world, we are teaching science.

The following science skills are appropriate for instruction with young children. You will be helping children use these skills as you pursue your study.

☐ *Observing*: Using any of the five senses to become aware of objects

☐ *Following directions*: Listening to or reading step-by-step directions and carrying them out

☐ *Classifying*: Arranging objects or information in groups according to some method

☐ *Creating models*: Portraying information through multisensory representations

☐ *Manipulating materials*: Handling materials safely and effectively

☐ *Measuring*: Making quantitative observations (time, temperature, weight, length, etc.)

☐ *Using numbers*: Applying mathematical rules

☐ *Asking questions*: Verbally demonstrating curiosity

☐ *Finding information*: Locating words, pictures, or numbers

☐ *Making predictions*: Suggesting what may happen (Predictions should come after children have some experiences with the topic. Predictions should be based on previously gathered data.)

☐ *Designing investigations*: Coming up with a plan to find out information or answers to questions

☐ *Communicating or recording information*: Communicating or recording information by the following:
   • talking to the teacher and/or other children
   • playing with theme-related props
   • drawing pictures
   • labeling
   • making diagrams
   • making graphs
   • writing (descriptive in learning logs or narrative)
   • taking photographs
   • recording on audio or videotape

☐ *Drawing conclusions*: Coming to various conclusions based on their stage of cognitive growth and their prior experiences

☐ *Applying knowledge*: Finding ways to use what is learned

About this book

Each chapter starts with a science goal to guide the parents and teachers. The goal is followed by ideas on how to plan for the activities, as well as lists of visual aids and related words that can be used for discussion.

Safety symbols, or icons, have been placed in the text to alert parents and teachers about activities that require supervision or other precautions.

 Scissors

 Adult supervision

Discussion Ideas, Activity Ideas, and Science Skills are also indicated by symbols in the text:

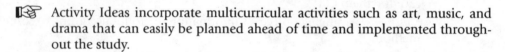 Discussion Ideas include questions for discussion that the teacher can ask the children.

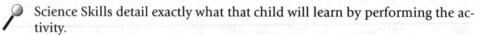 Activity Ideas incorporate multicurricular activities such as art, music, and drama that can easily be planned ahead of time and implemented throughout the study.

Science Skills detail exactly what that child will learn by performing the activity.

Pollen Point and Let's Create are interspersed throughout the text. Pollen Point contains interesting tidbits of information to be passed along verbally to the children or instructional information for the teacher or parent. Let's Create includes directions and simple patterns so the children can build actual models of the animals being studied. Children personify objects quite naturally; they enjoy giving their models names and personalities as they use them in a variety of ways. All of the Let's Create ideas can be embellished with a child's creative thoughts of how an animal might look or behave. The models can then be used in preplanned activities as well as spontaneous play.

A final word

For parents and teachers, every moment is an opportunity to teach science. By using this book, children will experience real plant life, create models to help them understand this life, and conduct a variety of activities that will enhance their knowledge. As each child moves from the real to the semi-concrete to the symbolic, he or she gains a true understanding of plants in our world. We hope the children enjoy studying seeds, flowers, and trees as they perform the activities in this book. More importantly, we hope that their sensitivity to life in their world will be enhanced.

Seeds

Science goals

To help children become aware of what seeds are and their usefulness to our lives

Planning

Send a note home to inform parents about this topic of study. Ask them to help their children collect all types of seeds to bring to class, and ask them to send empty egg cartons for sorting. Also ask them to send a white handkerchief or a piece of cotton material about 10–12 inches square. This material will serve as an observation mat and as a special "Seed Pouch" that each child can carry his seeds around in.

Each child will need a piece of colorful yarn to tie around his pouch. Prepare a center area for the study. Have magnifying glasses and informational books available. The center should have paper, pencils, and magic markers for labeling. Prepare to write words and/or sentences about seeds on a large sheet of chart paper.

Materials needed for discussion and activities

☐ Informational books
☐ Seeds
☐ Fresh fruits
☐ Fresh vegetables
☐ Nuts
☐ White handkerchiefs
☐ Colorful yarn
☐ Egg cartons
☐ Magnifying glasses
☐ Paper, pencils, magic markers
☐ Chart paper
☐ Plain white paper
☐ Construction paper
☐ Glue or tape
☐ Small cups

Related words

plant A living thing that does not have the ability to move from place to place and may be able to produce its own food. A plant grows and changes.

seed A part of a plant that is capable of producing a new plant

fruit A seed-bearing, edible part of a plant that comes from a flowering plant that usually lives for several or more years without being replanted

nut An edible seed that is part of a fruit with a hard shell. A nut can also be a one-celled fruit that has a hard shell (like an acorn).

vegetable A nutritious food that comes from the leaves, roots, flowers, seeds, or stems of certain plants that live for only one growing season and must be replanted each time. Note: A watermelon is often called a fruit but may be regarded as a vegetable because it grows on a vine that must be replanted each growing season. Varying definitions for vegetable exist.

 ## Activity idea: Seed journal

 ## Science skills
Recording information

Before you begin your study, create some type of journal that the children can record information in. One simple way to make a journal is to staple five or more sheets of plain white paper together with colorful construction paper for the front and back. Write or let the children write "Seeds" on the cover. Each day the children can record drawings, their own sentences about whatever was studied, or you can write as they dictate to you. After the journal is complete, you could let them glue seeds onto the cover to create a design or to just show a variety of seeds and their names.

Let's create a walnut shell rabbit
Buy walnuts at the grocery store to make a tiny bunny. (See Fig. 1-1.)

■ **1-1** *A walnut shell rabbit.*

 ## Science skills
Following directions, manipulating materials

What you need
- ☐ A bag of walnuts
- ☐ Butter knife to open walnuts
- ☐ Brown, white, and pink construction paper
- ☐ Scissors
- ☐ Glue
- ☐ Paper punch

☐ Cotton ball
☐ Black marker

 Directions

1. Open a walnut by inserting a butter knife in the large end of the nut and pulling the knife along the seam to force it into two halves. You will need a perfect half for each bunny.

2. Use the pattern (Fig. 1-2); trace and cut out two front legs, two back legs, and two ears.

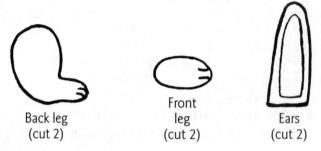

Back leg
(cut 2)

Front
leg
(cut 2)

Ears
(cut 2)

■ **1-2** *The patterns for the walnut shell rabbit.*

3. Glue the two front legs under one end of the shell, partly sticking out.

4. Glue a back leg on each side of the shell near the back.

5. Add two white paper punch eyes. Draw on eyeballs with a black marker.

6. Glue on two ears, a tiny pink paper snip for a nose, and two tiny square front teeth.

7. Glue on a tiny piece of cotton for a tail.

Let's create a seed mosaic

Beans, peas, and spices from the grocery store come in beautiful colors. You can add you own seeds to this project by drying seeds from melons, pumpkins, and other fruits and vegetables. (See Fig. 1-3 for a sample seed mosaic.)

 ## Science skills

Observing the differences among seeds, following directions, manipulating materials

What you need

☐ Newspapers to cover table
☐ Construction paper
☐ Crayons
☐ At least three dried seeds of different colors, such as peas, beans, popcorn, grass seed, bird seed, watermelon seeds, and pumpkin seeds
☐ White glue
☐ 11-×-13-inch plastic kitchen storage bags
☐ Cellophane tape

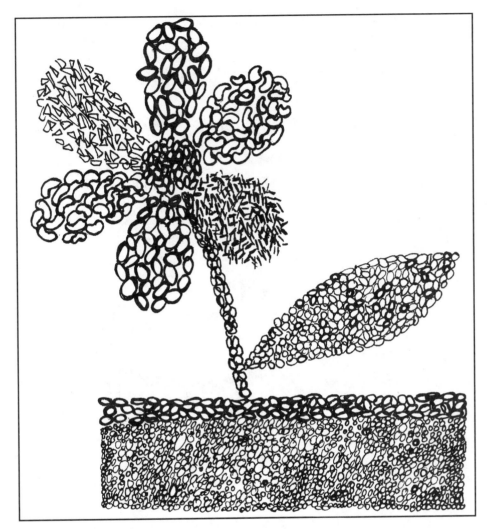

■ **1-3** *A seed mosaic.*

☐ Paper punch
☐ Yarn

Directions

1. Cover the table with newspaper to catch spilled seeds.
2. Use crayons to draw any sort of picture on the construction paper.
3. Spread glue on part of the finished picture. Pour one type of seed on the glue. Turn the picture on end, dumping the seed off. Some will stick to the glue on the picture.
4. Spread glue on another part of the picture. Pour a different seed on the glue. Repeat until your picture has many different seed textures and designs.
5. Let the picture lay flat overnight to dry. The next day, slip the picture into a plastic kitchen storage bag. Fold the end of the bag over and seal it with tape to hold in loose seeds.

6. To hang the picture, punch two holes in the top edge and add a piece of yarn.

7. If the picture bends and cannot be hung, tape a strip of heavy cardboard (you can get strips of cardboard by cutting up a box) just below the holes to hold it straight.

Let's create Mr. Seed Puppet
See Fig. 1-4 for a picture of what Mr. Seed Puppet should look like.

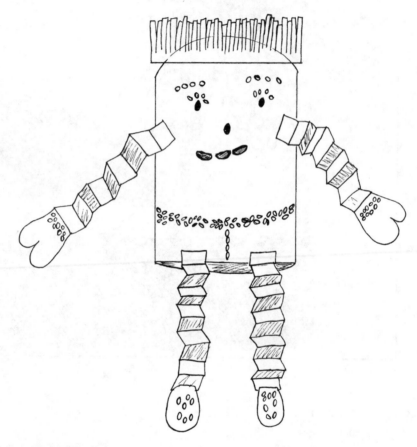

■ **1-4** *Mr. Seed Puppet.*

 ## Science skills
Finding, recording, and communicating information, measuring, following directions, manipulating materials

What you need
☐ 9- ×-12-inch construction paper (Felt may be used to make a cloth puppet.)

☐ White glue (To make a cloth puppet, use fabric glue.)

☐ Scissors

☐ Ruler

☐ Seeds of all kinds (We used three types of beans, split peas, rice, popcorn, and bird seed.

 Directions

1. Fold the sheet of construction paper (or felt) toward the center, 3 inches on each side (Fig. 1-5).

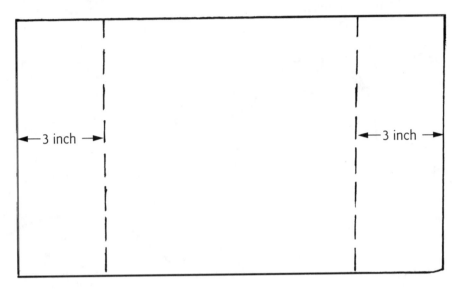

←— 3 inch —→   ←— 3 inch —→

■ **1-5** *Fold the paper over three inches on each side.*

2. Overlap the edges just a little and glue the seam down the middle. Cut one end in a rounded shape so it looks like a mitten (Fig. 1-6).

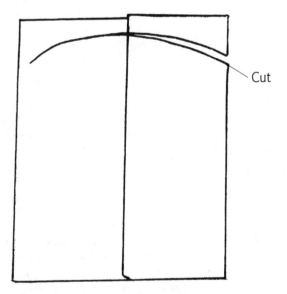

Cut

■ **1-6** *Cut one end in a rounded shape.*

3. Use a ruler to measure and cut four strips of construction paper (or felt) to make arms and legs for your puppet. Pleat the paper strips. Glue the arms and legs on the puppet.

4. To make hair for your puppet, use a ruler to measure and cut a rectangle 2¼ × 6 inches. Fringe the rectangle and glue it on the puppet's head.

5. Use the patterns in Fig. 1-7 to trace and cut out hands and feet. Glue them on the puppet.

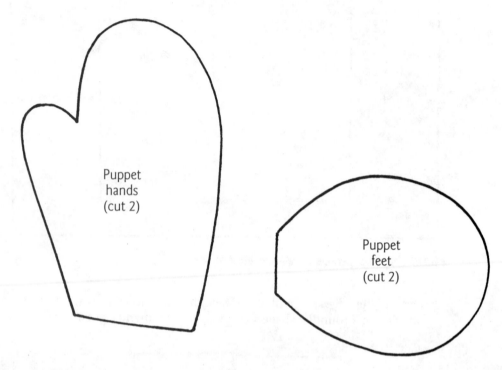

Puppet
hands
(cut 2)

Puppet
feet
(cut 2)

■ **1-7** *The patterns for Mr. Seed Puppet's hands and feet.*

6. Glue seeds on the puppet to make his eyes, nose, mouth, and clothes. Lay him flat until the glue dries.

7. Use Mr. Seed Puppet to tell your classmates some things that you have learned about seeds. Perhaps you can write (or tell) a story or skit for Mr. Seed Puppet about the importance of seeds.

Before you talk about seeds, you will need to provide experiences and talk about what a plant is.

Provide a real plant to show the children. Provide a plant which has roots. Show the children the flower (if there is one), the leaves, the stem, and the roots. An excellent plant to show is a strawberry plant. You may be able to find one that has the delicate white flowers, which become green strawberries, which become red strawberries. You can provide a strawberry for the children to examine (or enough strawberries that each child can eat one). The children can then see the seeds on a strawberry. If these seeds were planted, new strawberry plants would grow. A sunflower is another excellent type of plant to show to children. The seeds are in the middle of the flower.

Scientists divide living things into two main groups: plants and animals. Animals move about, but most plants stay in one place once they start to grow. Animals have to find their food, but plants are able to make their own food by using air, sunlight, and water. Plants supply people with many things they need, like food. For example, apples comes from apple trees. Plants provide shelter and homes. Wood from trees is used in building homes and making furniture. Even many kinds of medicines are made from plants.

Many plants produce seeds. Seeds are one of nature's smallest and most productive forms of life. Seeds are the end of life for some plants and the beginning of life for others. What is a seed? A seed is a part of a plant that is able to produce a new plant. Inside every seed there is a tiny, baby plant waiting to come out. There are many kinds, sizes, and shapes of seeds. If you know what kind of plant a seed comes from, you know what it will grow into. An apple seed will grow into an apple tree.

Pollen Point

Most seeds begin inside a flower. The center part of a flower is the pistil. *At the bottom of the pistil are egg cells. Around the pistil are stamens, which make a yellow powder called* pollen. *Pollen must reach an egg cell for a seed to be made. After a grain of pollen lands on the pistil, it may travel down the long tube and join an egg cell. Flowers can use their own pollen or pollen from other flowers to make seeds. When a flower dies, new seeds are growing. The seeds may fall off or a pod or fruit may grow around seeds to protect them.*

☞ **Activity idea: Where can we find seeds? In fruits**

 Science skills
Observing, classifying

It is very important to help children discover where seeds can be found in fruits. Decide on various fruits that you can bring in to show the children where seeds can be found. You may want each child to bring a type of fruit on a certain day for the lesson.

For example, use an apple. Show them the whole apple. Now cut a small piece off the side. Ask the children if they see any seeds. Now keep cutting off slices until the children see seeds. Ask them where the seeds are in the apple. (Answer: "In the middle"). Now do the same with a grape, orange, lemon, lime, watermelon, tomato, or whatever fruits you have. You can lead them to discover that these fruits actually protect the seeds within them. "Do we eat the seeds from the apple?" "Do we eat the seeds from the grape?" "Do we eat the seeds from the orange?" If you are able to have a peach or plum, the children will enjoy finding the pit which actually encases the seed. Break open the pit and find the seed.

Peanut plants produce a fruit. (A peanut plant does not quite fit our definition of a fruit, but there is more than one way that a fruit can be defined.) The whole peanut is the fruit and inside are usually two seeds. If possible, let each child have peanuts in their shells. Let them remove the shell and break apart each peanut. Use a magnifying glass to find the embryo. Find peanut in an encyclopedia. Show the children a picture of the plant and how the peanuts are under the ground.

Students will enjoy looking at and eating seeds from fruits in which the seeds are soft and flavorful enough to eat. Look at and taste a banana or kiwi.

Ask the children "Can you think of a fruit that has the seeds on the outside?" Show a strawberry and talk about the seeds. Let the children taste as many fruits as possible.

Save the seeds that you do not eat. Wash them and lay them out on paper towels to dry. Use the egg cartons for sorting the seeds. Label the egg carton "Seeds From Fruits."

 ## Activity idea: Where can we find seeds? In vegetables
Plan to bring or have the children bring vegetables for seed finding. Some good choices are: cucumbers, okra, beans, peas, squash, green pepper, and corn.

Cut the vegetables open so the children can see the seeds. Taste each food if appropriate. Talk about how the seeds feel. Are they hard or soft? What colors are the seeds? Wash any seeds that you want to keep and let them dry on a paper towel. Use an egg carton for sorting the seeds. Label the egg carton "Seeds From Vegetables."

Activity idea: Vegetable printing to show seeds

Science skills
Recording information

You will need several tin plates with liquid paint poured on the bottom. You will need white construction paper. You will need vegetables and a knife (just for the adult) to cut the vegetables in half. The child will dip the cut side of the vegetable in the paint and then press it on the paper to make a print that will show the seeds. Some vegetables that work well are green or red peppers, squash, okra, and corn.

 ## Activity idea: Where can we find seeds? On trees

Science skills
Observing, classifying

Spring and Fall are excellent times to find seeds from trees. Plan to take a walk outdoors when trees are just beginning to get new leaves. Look for seeds on the trees. Look on the ground for seeds. Try to decide where the seeds came from. Collect some to bring back to the room. Maple seeds are so pretty as they fly through the air. Acorns from oak trees are wonderful to collect. Pine cones hold many seeds. Magnolia trees have beautiful seeds. Enjoy looking for seeds on the trees in your area.

Nuts are seeds that can grow on trees. You may have such trees in your area (pecan, hazelnut, almond, walnut).

Use an egg carton to sort the seeds. Label the egg carton "Seeds From Trees."

Activity idea: Where can we find seeds? On other kinds of plants

 ### Science skills
Finding information

Here are some seeds that come from plants that you probably will not be able to observe. You will need to have encyclopedias and other informational books available for children to look at pictures.

Cereal grains: wheat, rice, corn

Spices: nutmeg, pepper, dill, vanilla, caraway, mustard

Seeds used for drinks: coffee, cocoa

 ## Activity idea: Where can we find seeds? At a pet store or bird supply store

 ### Science skills
Observing, finding information

Pet stores have all kinds of seeds that mice, hamsters, gerbils, and birds eat. Bird supply stores have great selections of seeds to feed birds and animals like squirrels and chipmunks in your yard. If possible, visit these places. If you cannot go, ask parents to send seeds that they may have to feed their pets or birds. The children will enjoy looking at these. You may want to put a bird feeder in your schoolyard and feed birds on a regular basis. By feeding birds, the children will learn about a variety of seeds that different birds enjoy.

Activity idea: Where can we find seeds? Many places

Science skills
Observing, finding information

Seeds may be found on the ground, on your clothes, and a variety of other places. Seeds may float, fly, tumble, roll, or hang on things and move with them. Seeds may travel by wind, water, and with the help of animals. Maple seeds look like little propellers as they whirl through the air. Dandelion seeds are easily carried by wind. Seeds may fall into lakes and streams and be carried to other places. Animals help carry seeds. Squirrels bury acorns and many of these later sprout into oak trees. Crows eat fruits and then throw seeds out of their mouths. Some animals eat fruits and deposit the undigested seeds on the ground as part of the animal's waste. Wading birds in ponds and lakes carry seeds on their muddy feet.

 ## Activity idea: What will I be when I grow up?

 ### Science skills
Asking questions, communicating information, applying knowledge

Plan a play about seeds. The title will be "What Will I Be When I Grow Up?." Choose five children to be seeds that you have studied. For example, one child might be an apple seed, one a sunflower seed, one an acorn, etc. Each child should make a costume from a paper bag to wear. Choose five other children to be the corresponding adult plants. For example, one child would be an apple tree, one a sunflower plant, one an oak tree, etc. The grown-up plants will need to wear a poster board costume to show the plant they represent. For example, an apple tree could be drawn and colored on poster board and the child could use yarn to wear the poster around his neck. Each seed should have a turn to ask the question. Afterwards the correct adult plant will respond by telling a story about how it grew into the plant. It is important to let each child use the knowledge they have gained to come up with a wonderful story of where the seed grew, who cared for it, and the food or beauty or shelter it has provided. Here is an example of how one episode might go:

The apple seed will ask: "What will I be when I grow up?"

The apple tree might say: "If you get enough water, air, sunlight, and you have good soil to live in, you will grow up to be an apple tree like me. I once started out as a little seed just like you. A farmer planted me. His little boy watered me and made sure I got sun and fresh air. At first I was a little plant, but I kept growing and growing. Soon I was taller than the boy and then taller than the farmer. I have pretty flowers in the spring which then turn to red apples." (etc.)

☞ Activity idea: Where can we find seeds? At the grocery store

 ## Science skills
Observing, finding information, recording information

If it is possible, visit a grocery store. The children will have fun looking for seeds and foods that are made with seeds. Here are some foods you want to see and talk about:

fruits	cookies
vegetables	cereals
nuts (pecans, walnuts, peanuts)	rice
popcorn	coffee
beans	spices
peas	peanut butter
breads	chocolate
cakes	

If the children are able to write, send them along with their journals and pencils. Let them write the names of all the items that have or use seeds in any way.

Seeds help feed the world. What would the world be like if we couldn't use seeds for food? We would not have bread, or cookies, or peanut butter, or chocolate frosting. From seeds we can create all kinds of delicious foods to eat. We should be very thankful for seeds.

Let's create a cereal box book

Cereal boxes contain so much information! They tell you not only what's in the box, but also where the cereal is made, the date it was boxed, how much one person is expected to eat (serving size), and lots more! Let's find out about cereal by creating this book. See Fig. 1-8.

■ **1-8** *The cereal box book. To add the stapled pages, glue the first page and the last page onto the inside book cover.*

 ## Science skills

Finding, recording, and communicating information, following directions, manipulating materials

What you need
☐ An empty cereal box
☐ Scissors
☐ Construction paper
☐ White glue
☐ 10 pages of copy paper or notebook paper
☐ Stapler

 #### Directions

1. Open the cereal box at both ends and the side and lay it out flat as shown in Fig. 1-9.
2. Cut off the box flaps. They are shaded in Fig. 1-9. Save them. They contain interesting data that you can investigate later.

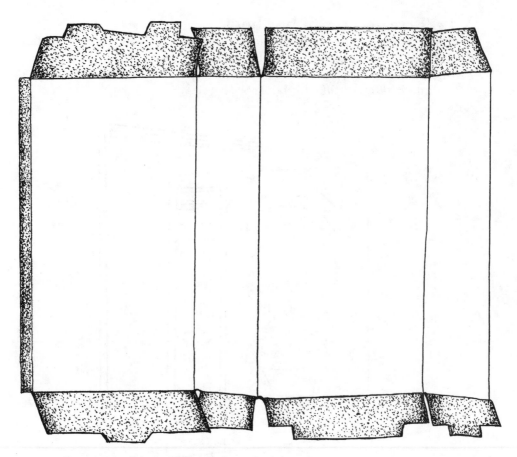

■ **1-9** *Cut off the box flaps which are shaded.*

3. Fold the box in half (like a book!) so the edges are even.

4. Line the inside of your book with construction paper by using the book as a pattern. Lay the book on the construction paper and trace around it. Cut out the construction paper and glue a piece inside the front and the back of the book.

5. Cut ten sheets of copy paper or notebook paper so they fit inside the book. Staple them together close to one edge (Fig. 1-10).

6. Real books are glued together. To glue the pages in your book, open the cereal box book cover out flat. Spread glue on the first page of copy paper. Glue the copy paper inside the front cover. Keeping the book flat, spread glue on the last page of the copy paper. Glue the copy paper inside the back cover. Let the book lay flat to dry.

7. After the glue has dried close the book, pressing it flat with any heavy object such as a block.

Some suggested activities for the Cereal Box Book

The Cereal Box Book could be used as a journal to record any information that interests you. Just by investigating the book's cover and the box flaps, you can find out about the following things and record them in your book:

☐ How much did the cereal weigh? What do those weights mean?

☐ What seeds are included in the cereal? What other ingredients are listed?

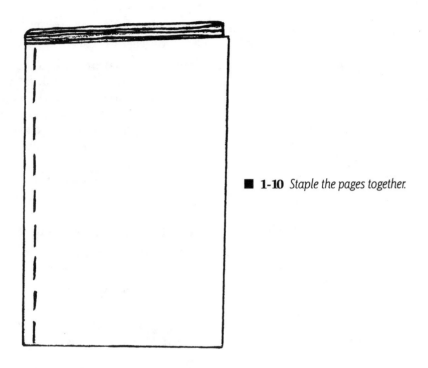

■ **1-10** *Staple the pages together.*

☐ Look at the nutrition facts on the box. Compare some of the facts on your box of cereal with the cereals your classmates have chosen.

☐ Who made the cereal? Where was it made? Can you find its place of origin on a map?

☐ When was the cereal made? Does it have a freshness date?

☐ Does your cereal have a patent number? What does this patent mean?

☐ Find all the adjectives used to describe the cereal!

☞ Activity idea: Let's look at seeds

Science skills
Observing, asking questions

You will need a large piece of poster board or chart paper, glue or clear tape, and a magic marker. You will need about 5–10 different kinds of seeds, but enough of each kind so that you can give one to every child. (If you have packets purchased from a nursery, you will probably have plenty of seeds.)

Let the children sit on the floor in a circle. Ask each child to lay his handkerchief unfolded and flat in front of him. This will serve as an observation mat for the seeds. (Put the child's name on the back of the handkerchief with a piece of masking tape.) Give each child a magnifying glass. Tell the children that you will give each one of them a certain kind of seed and that they should look at it with their magnifying glass. Perhaps you begin with apple seeds. Give each child one and allow time for looking and conversation between the children.

Write the title "Seeds" on your chart. Below that write "apple seed" and glue or tape an apple seed to the chart. As the children talk to you about the seed, write words or sentences on the chart to tell about the seed. The sentences might tell about the color, size, shape, or feel of the seed.

Repeat this with all of the types of seeds. After you are finished, ask each child to put his seeds in the middle of the handkerchief and pull all sides of the handkerchief up and tie the pouch up with a piece of yarn. Help the children tie a bow with the yarn. Each child can now carry his own pouch of seeds. Whenever a child wants to look at his seeds, he can just untie the yarn, open the handkerchief, and spread the seeds out for viewing, perhaps with a magnifying glass.

A seed is made up of three parts. One part is called the embryo. The embryo is a plant in its first stage of development. (A human being is called an embryo during the first few months of development before birth.) The embryo is alive and has the first root, stem, and leaves of a new plant.

Another part of a seed is the cotyledons. These are special leaflike structures which absorb and use food.

Another part of the seed is the seed coat. It is the covering for the seed and protects the seed.

If there is a tiny, living plant inside each seed, how can we make this plant come out? There is food inside the seed. How can we help the embryo use it?

☞ Activity idea: How can we make the tiny plant come out?

 ## Science skills

Designing investigations, drawing conclusions, applying knowledge

Get two clear glass or plastic containers. Label one Container "With Water" (#1) and the other container "No water" (#2). Line them both with paper towels. Put one or two tablespoons of water in the #1 container. Put the same type of seed in each container, placed between the paper and the glass.

Let the children watch what happens over several days. Give the children the opportunity to draw conclusions about what happens. Guide them in concluding that the water softened the food so the embryo could use it and the embryo came out. After sprouting, oxygen from the air enters the seed and combines with the food to cause a plant to grow. Water, oxygen, and warmth are needed to help a plant develop. The water softens the food inside the seed so that the embryo can use it. The embryo can live off of the food stored in the seed for a short time. Guide them in seeing that the roots grow downward and the leaves and stem grow upward toward the sunlight.

> ### *Pollen Point*
>
> *Controlling variables is very important in science. In this prior activity, it is very important to keep everything the same except the water.*
>
> *After doing this experiment, you can put different kinds of seeds in a wet paper towel lined container to see the differences in sprouting among various kinds of seeds.*

Another way to watch seeds sprout is to use a long metal pan. Line it with wet paper towels. Lay seeds on the wet paper towels (popcorn and peanuts are good choices). Add extra water to make sure there is plenty of moisture. Cover the pan with clear plastic wrap. Watch what happens each day.

Here is another activity you can do to help the children understand the importance of water for seeds.

 ## Activity idea: Seeds and water

 ### Science skills
Observing, making predictions

Let children predict what they think will happen to seeds that have no water and those that do. You will need some beans or peas. You can buy a bag of one kind or you can buy a bag of mixed beans (used for making mixed bean soup). Get two small, clear containers (medicine containers might be good). Fill each container half full of beans or peas. Add water to cover the seeds in one container. Let the other container remain dry. Let the children make predictions about what they think will happen. Within 24 hours the seeds in the container of water will have swollen and filled the container. The other seeds will remain unchanged. Be sure to let the children discover all of this before you explain it. Give them plenty of time to talk about what they are doing and seeing.

Pour the water off of the seeds and let the children handle these. They will see that the seed coat will be easy to remove and they can break the seeds apart and examine them with magnifying glasses. Let the children also hold the dry seeds. Talk about the differences between the wet seeds and the dry seeds.

Would you rather carry a cornfield around in your pocket or a bag of corn from which that field could grow? When the Pilgrims arrived in the New World, aboard the Mayflower in 1620, they brought seeds to plant gardens in the spring. Although they were very hungry aboard ship, they kept the seeds to start their own gardens. The Native Americans who were already here in America, showed the Pilgrims how to plant corn. The Pilgrims could then have corn as a vegetable, popcorn, and cornbread.

 ## Activity idea: Let's play with seeds

 ### Science skills
Observing, following directions, using numbers, making predictions, designing investigations, communicating and recording information, drawing conclusions

Tell the children that you want them to think of games that could be played with seeds. You may want to let them pretend they live in the time of the Pilgrims when no toys could be purchased. Give children plenty of time to think of creative ideas, individually or as groups. Let them write their ideas on paper or dictate them to you. If they need to make something to go with the seeds, give them time to do that. Here are some games to play to get things started:

1. "Find the Seed." One child hides a seed while the other children close their eyes. Selected children can try to find the seed. Whoever finds it can hide it next. (Choose a large seed that will be easily recognized.)

2. "Which Hand Has The Seed?" Partners play this game. The two people stand or sit facing each other. One person holds the seed behind his back and hides the seed in one of his hands. He then holds out both hands, fingers closed and up. The other person taps the hand he thinks the seed is in. The person with the seed opens both hands to reveal where the seed is. The other person now has a turn to hold the seed.

3. "How Many Seeds?" Partners can play this game. Pour seeds into a small bowl. They can be the same kind of seeds or a mixture. The children take turns taking a handful of seeds out of the bowl. Before the child lays the seeds down on the table or floor, they both estimate how many seeds there will be. After the child lays the seeds down, they can count them and see who came closer.

   You can also play this game with a tablespoon and estimate how many seeds will fit in the tablespoon.

4. "Seed Toss." Place a bucket or large bowl on the floor. Let the children line up, with the first person about three or four feet from the container. Place a piece of colored tape on the floor as a place to stand. Give each child one seed. Each child gets to stand on the tape and try to throw his seed into the container. After everyone has had a turn, count the seeds in the container. Now count the seeds on the floor that missed the container. Add the two together. You should get an answer that equals the number of children who participated.

5. "Seed Tic Tac Toe." Play this old favorite except use one kind of seed for the X's and one kind for the O's.

6. "Who's Got The Seed?" All of the children sit in a circle. One person is given a seed. When music is played, the seed is passed to the right from one person's hand to the next. When the music stops, the children say, "Who's got the seed?" That person stands up, gives the seed to the person on her right and then sits in the middle of the circle. The music starts again and the seed is passed. When five people get in the middle of the circle the game is over.

7. "Let's Add". Purchase a bag of dry, large lima beans. Let the children paint one side of each bean a specific color, perhaps blue. Each child gets ten beans (or any selected number) which he puts into a cup. He pours his beans out on a table and then writes an addition problem according to how many beans show blue and how many show white.

8. "Let's Subtract." Follow the same format as in game No. 7 except this time, take away the beans with the colored side showing and then write a subtraction problem.

9. "Watermelon Seeds." Make large watermelon slices from colored construction paper. Cut out watermelon seeds from black construction paper. For each slice of watermelon you will need 15 seeds. To begin the game, each person puts all 15 watermelon seeds on the watermelon slice. Each player in turn rolls a dice. The player then removes that number of

seeds from his watermelon slice. Play continues until all players have been able to take away all of the seeds from their slice.

Activity idea: Indoor garden

Science skills

Following directions, creating models, manipulating materials, recording information, applying knowledge

You can plant an indoor garden in a small plastic child's swimming pool or a container like a turkey roasting pan. Fill the container with potting soil. Plant various kinds of seeds, like grass seeds, carrot seeds, and flower seeds. Use small rocks to divide the garden into sections and label the seed areas with little flags on toothpicks. You can add small plastic animals and people to live and work in the garden. Include a spray bottle of water nearby so the children can water the garden each day. Place the garden near a window so it can get sunlight.

Activity idea: Closure: Let's plant seeds

Science skills

Manipulating materials, applying knowledge

Review your initial goals and help children apply their knowledge to plant seeds to grow. Think about the long-term plan for the seeds you will plant. Do you want to plant them in cups, let them sprout, and then send them home? Or do you want to eventually plant the young plants outdoors to create a flower or vegetable garden? In the next chapter we will be talking about a flower garden, so you might want to plan ahead for that. If we want the little plant within the seed to grow well, we need to provide soil, light, and water. You will need to select some seeds that you want to plant. You will need small containers and potting soil or compressed peat pellets. (Compressed peat pellets swell up when you add water and then you can insert a seed in the middle. They make planting seeds very easy because no soil gets spilled.) You will need a spray bottle filled with water.

Help the children plant the seeds, label the containers, and water with the spray bottle. Place the containers in a location where they can get some sunlight. Let the children water the seeds each day. If the children are keeping a Seed Journal, help them record information each day. After the seeds have sprouted, decide what you want to do with the young plants.

It is so much fun to plant grass seed and then watch the grass grow. You will need a large pan or container that is not too deep (no more than 2 inches deep). Fill the pan with potting soil. Sprinkle grass seed over the top. Spray water on each day with a spray bottle. Before long, you will have grass growing. The children can enjoy watching it grow. They can cut the grass with scissors. They can put plastic animals and people in the grass for play activities.

Activity idea: Creative dramatization of a seed sprouting

 ## Science skills

Following directions, communicating information

It will be fun and meaningful to let the children act out a story of a seed sprouting. It is important to let the children help decide how to act this out, based on what they have observed through the prior experiences from this book. The actors you will need are:

- ☐ someone to plant the seed
- ☐ a seed
- ☐ raindrops
- ☐ sun
- ☐ air

The person who is the seed will need a large brown paper grocery bag to put over his head. This will be the seed coat. The soil will be represented by paper. Get a large piece of brown craft paper (about 6 feet long and three feet wide). Cut a slit about 2 feet long in the middle. Let the children decide how they should dress to be raindrops and the sun. They will have creative ideas for this.

Tell a story and allow the children to dramatize it, using their own creative ideas. The story could go like this:

Once there was a little sunflower seed. A young girl named Helen decided to plant the seed in the ground. (The seed should curl up on the floor with the brown paper bag over his head. Next, lay the brown piece of craft paper over the seed with the slit directly over the bag. This will allow the seed to sprout up through the soil.)

She watered the seed with her watering can each day for three days. (You could call out specific days of the week by name, like Sunday, Monday, and Tuesday. The watering can could have little bits of blue paper that could fall onto the craft paper ground.) The sun shone brightly down on the little seed in the ground.

The next day it rained. (Raindrops should gently fall on the ground.) Then the sun came out to shine on the seed in the ground.

The next day the seed sprouted. It pushed up through the soil (the seed should come up through the slit in the paper). The seed coat came off. (The child should push the paper bag off his head.) Little leaves appeared. (The child could hold his hands upward.)

The little girl continued to water the plant and the rain fell on it and the sun shone on it and the air nourished it. (Whoever is the air can creatively act here.)

The plant continued to grow and grow into a beautiful sunflower. (The child could gradually stand up while growing.)

> ## *Pollen Point: Seeds feed the world!*
>
> *Russia relies on wheat, Mexico on corn and beans, Japan on rice. To emphasize the importance of seeds in the diet of the world's people, ask parents in your classroom to come in and fix a seed-based recipe from their family's heritage. A parent with an Australian background might make something containing wheat, for instance. A parent whose ancestors were from India might make a dish containing rice. Find those countries on a world map.*

Let's create a napkin apron

Each person can create an easy apron by glueing a large paper dinner napkin onto a white streamer "waistband". The children can decorate their aprons with markers. (See Fig. 1-11.)

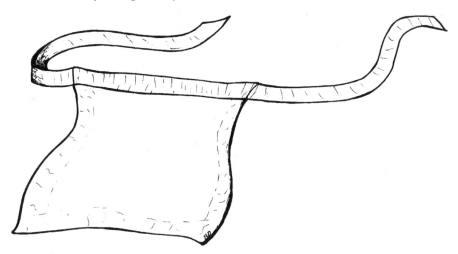

■ **1-11** *A napkin apron.*

 ## Science skills

Following directions, manipulating materials

What you need

☐ A large paper dinner napkin
☐ A white crepe paper streamer
☐ Glue
☐ Markers

Directions

1. Open the paper napkin into a large square.
2. Cut a white crepe paper streamer that is long enough to go around your waist two times.
3. Lay the napkin on newspapers and decorate it with markers. Color it carefully so that the napkin doesn't tear.

4. Glue one edge of the napkin in the middle of the crepe paper streamer "waist band."

5. Lay it flat to dry overnight. The next day you can wear your own apron when you cook.

The value of cooking with children

Because cooking involves learning and using math facts, following written or spoken directions, observing physical and chemical changes that occur in food, asking questions and discovering answers, science process skills take a front row seat in the classroom kitchen. In fact when we cook with children we introduce them to a whole realm of learning opportunities. Four of these are listed below.

☐ **Cooking activities help a child practice and learn socialization skills.** When a child cooks with other children, she practices turn-taking, sharing and cooperation as she and her classmates use various ingredients and tools. She gains the social skill of discussion, learning from and teaching other children. She can also gain an appreciation of ethnic diversity if her teacher enlists parent volunteers to come into the classroom and help the children prepare foods from a different region or country.

☐ **Cooking activities help a child practice and learn school-ready skills.** As a child mixes, spreads, cuts, separates eggs, and combines ingredients he practices small motor skills and eye-hand coordination that will aid him in learning to write letters and numbers when he is ready to do so. He engages in pre-reading skills as he realizes that the rebus chart created by the teacher actually lets everyone know what to do next in a recipe. He uses math as he counts, measures, and pours. In order to complete the creation of an interesting food, he finds it necessary to listen, follow directions, and develop self control, just as he will need to do in any elementary classroom.

☐ **Cooking validates a child's sense of self-worth.** Following a recipe to completion increases a child's sense of self esteem and self confidence. He feels success and pride as he shares with his friends the food he helped cook, and as he shares the recipe with his family.

☐ **Cooking activities can be incorporated into the whole day of the child.** Cooking can act as a springboard for making books and charts, using language skills to describe sequencing of events, and descriptive words to describe texture and taste. As children hold, cook, and taste various fruits, nuts, and vegetables they can learn about the importance of cleanliness as well as good nutrition. They can write food related journals and sing songs about peanut, peanut butter or any other food! Creating food mixtures and observing the chemical reactions that occur when individual ingredients turn into a totally new product help children understand the beginning elements of chemistry surrounding heat and cold, solids and liquids, and mixtures. As they follow a recipe they gain first-hand knowledge of fractions, and they learn the importance of accurate interpretation and measurement. For instance, what would happen to a cookie recipe if one teaspoon of salt were replaced with one tablespoon of salt? Such accidents happen during cooking events, and the results are unforgettable when the food is tasted.

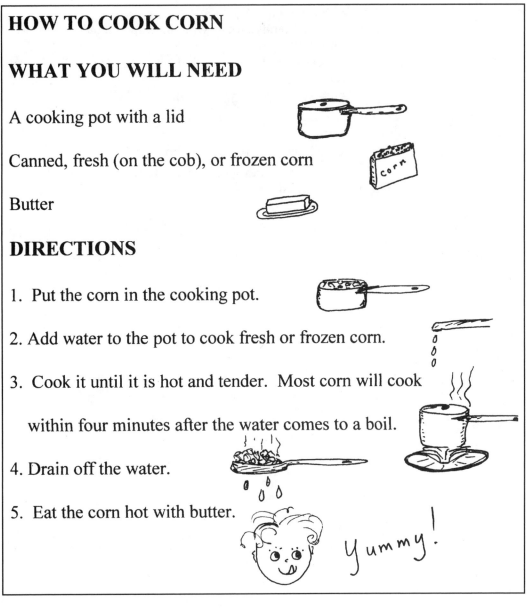

HOW TO COOK CORN

WHAT YOU WILL NEED

A cooking pot with a lid

Canned, fresh (on the cob), or frozen corn

Butter

DIRECTIONS

1. Put the corn in the cooking pot.

2. Add water to the pot to cook fresh or frozen corn.

3. Cook it until it is hot and tender. Most corn will cook

   within four minutes after the water comes to a boil.

4. Drain off the water.

5. Eat the corn hot with butter.

Yummy!

■ **1-12** *Rebus chart for cooking corn.*

 Safety First: When cooking with children, always consider their safety first. An adult must supervise all activities, making certain that the children are not harmed by hot stoves and sharp utensils.

Appliances for cooking in the classroom
The following electric appliances can be used to cook many of these recipes in the classroom:

☐ Electric skillet for pancakes, Johnny cakes, anything fried.

☐ Toaster oven for baking six cupcakes or muffins at a time, a few pretzels, other small baking jobs.

- ☐ Electric corn popper for popping non-greasy popcorn.
- ☐ Single hot plate for heating liquids such as syrup for popcorn balls, soup, vegetables, and hot chocolate.
- ☐ Crock Pot or Slow Cooker for making soups that take all day to cook. Also good for keeping foods warm.
- ☐ Electric waffle iron for making Waffle Iron Cookies.
- ☐ Microwave ovens are sometimes available in the teachers' lounge for heating, cooking, melting.
- ☐ Full-size ovens are sometimes available in the school kitchen.

From seeds we can create pancakes and syrup, peanut butter toast, cupcakes with chocolate frosting, and fried rice. Seeds are an important food all over the world.

The Seed Cookbook

by Elizabeth Dondiego

Corn recipes

Corn cereal

Look in the grocery store for breakfast cereal made from corn. We found Corn Pops®, Corn Flakes®, and Corn Chex®. There are lots more. Some cereals, such as Cookie Crisp®, are made of four seeds: corn, rice, wheat, and oats!

Popcorn and popcorn balls

Popcorn is a dried seed. Water that's trapped inside each kernel changes to steam when the popcorn is heated. It turns the seed inside out with an explosive POP. This recipe uses three seed foods: popcorn, corn syrup, and peanut butter.

What you need

- ☐ Electric hot air popcorn popper
- ☐ Popcorn
- ☐ ½ cup corn syrup
- ☐ ¼ cup sugar
- ☐ ½ cup peanut butter
- ☐ Margarine

Directions

1. Pop the popcorn in the electric hot air popper by following the directions that come with the machine.
2. Pour the popcorn in a bowl and remove the kernels that didn't pop.
3. Measure the corn syrup and sugar into a saucepan. Cook over medium heat, stirring constantly, until the mixture comes to a boil and the sugar is dissolved.
4. Remove the pan from the heat. Add the peanut butter and stir until smooth. Pour this syrup over the popped corn. Stir it until the corn is coated.

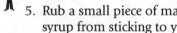

5. Rub a small piece of margarine between your hands to keep the sticky syrup from sticking to you. Pick up a handful of popcorn and squeeze it into a big ball.

Yield: 12 baseball-sized popcorn balls

Colored popcorn balls

The syrup for traditional colored popcorn balls must be cooked by an adult after the children measure the ingredients.

What you need

- ☐ Electric hot air popcorn popper
- ☐ Popcorn (You will need 10 cups of popped corn)
- ☐ A large bowl or baking pan
- ☐ Solid shortening
- ☐ A 2-quart saucepan
- ☐ Wooden spoon

- ☐ 1 cup sugar
- ☐ ⅓ cup water
- ☐ ⅓ cup molasses
- ☐ ¼ cup margarine (½ stick)
- ☐ 1 teaspoon salt
- ☐ 1 teaspoon vanilla
- ☐ Red, green, yellow, or blue liquid food coloring

Directions

1. Pop the popcorn in the electric hot air popper by following the directions that come with the machine.
2. The children can grease the large bowl or pan, using their fingers and solid shortening. Then they can measure the popcorn into the bowl, removing the kernels that didn't pop.
3. Help them measure the sugar, water, molasses, margarine, and salt into the saucepan. Now an adult must take over to prevent burns.
4. Cook over medium heat, stirring occasionally, until the sugar dissolves. Turn the heat to high and let the syrup come to a boil. Test it for doneness by dropping a small amount of syrup into a cup of cold water. The syrup will form a ball of candy in the bottom of the cup. Touch this ball with your finger. When the syrup is ready to use, it will form a hard ball in the cup of cold water. Continue testing the syrup as it cooks, until it reaches this hard-ball stage.
5. Remove the syrup from the heat. Stir in the vanilla and food coloring. Pour the hot syrup over the popped corn. The children can stir the corn with wooden spoons until each piece is coated. The syrup is very hot, so they must not touch it.
6. Give each child a small piece of shortening to rub on their hands. Then they can pick up the coated corn and shape it into balls the size of a baseball. The shortening will help prevent the syrup from burning them because it doesn't let the popcorn stick to their hands.

Yield: About ten popcorn balls

How to cook corn

Fresh corn is a delicious seed to eat. It can be cooked on a hot plate, in a slow cooker, or in a microwave oven. To emphasize that corn is a seed, students can create a rebus chart that combines pictures with words for beginning readers. The children should draw a picture beside each ingredient or direction. (See Fig. 1-12 for sample rebus.)

What you need
- ☐ A cooking pot with a lid
- ☐ Canned, fresh (on the cob), or frozen corn
- ☐ Butter

Directions
1. Put the corn in the cooking pot.
2. Add water to the pot to cook fresh or frozen corn.

3. Cook it until it is hot and tender. Most corn will cook within four minutes after the water comes to a boil.
4. Drain off the water.
5. Eat the corn hot with butter.

Johnny (Journey) Cakes

In the 1800s people who were going on a journey (a long trip) took a bag of ground corn with them. Sometimes they took a cow, too. At the end of a long day of walking or riding in a wagon, they mixed the cornmeal with milk and fried it in fat over a campfire. That's how Journey Cakes got their name. As time went by, the name changed to Johnny Cakes. In some parts of the United States today people hold contests to see who can cook the best Johnny Cakes.

What you need
- ☐ 1 egg
- ☐ 2 cups cornmeal
- ☐ 1½ teaspoons onion salt
- ☐ 1¼ cups milk
- ☐ Vegetable oil
- ☐ Butter or margarine

Directions
1. Beat the egg with a fork.
2. Stir in the cornmeal, salt, and milk to make a thick batter.
3. Heat vegetable oil in an electric skillet.
4. Drop spoonfuls of batter onto the hot skillet and fry to a golden brown on each side.
5. Serve Johnny Cakes hot with butter or margarine.

Yield: 2 dozen cakes

Cornmeal muffins

Before refrigerators were invented, milk didn't stay fresh for long. When it became sour it was used for baking wonderful breads and muffins such as these. This recipe uses buttermilk and came from the state of West Virginia. It uses two seeds; can you identify them?

What you need
- ☐ Solid shortening to grease the muffin cups
- ☐ ¼ cup vegetable oil
- ☐ 2 eggs
- ☐ ¾ cup buttermilk
- ☐ 1¾ cups cornmeal
- ☐ ¼ cup flour
- ☐ 4¼ cups sugar
- ☐ 1 teaspoon baking powder

☐ ½ teaspoon baking soda

☐ ½ teaspoon salt

Directions

1. Preheat the oven to 400°F. Grease the muffin cups with solid shortening. (These muffins stick to paper cupcake liners.)
2. In a large bowl, mix together the oil, eggs, and buttermilk until they are blended.
3. Stir in the cornmeal, flour, sugar, baking powder, baking soda, and salt.
4. Fill each muffin cup ¾ full of batter. Bake at 400°F. for about 20 minutes until golden brown.

Yield: 1 dozen muffins

How to make tortilla chips with salsa

Crispy chips dipped in salsa are a delicious snack. To emphasize that tortilla chips are made of corn seeds, students can create a rebus chart that combines pictures with words for beginning readers. The children should draw a picture beside each ingredient or direction.

What you need

☐ Tortilla chips

☐ Mild salsa

☐ Two bowls

Directions

1. Empty the chips into a bowl.
2. Pour the salsa into another bowl.
3. Dip a chip into the salsa and eat it.
4. Share the Chips and Salsa with your friends.

Fried cornmeal mush

Cornmeal mush has been eaten by Americans for hundreds of years. Native Americans introduced this dish to the European settlers. Chill the hot mush and fry it the next day.

What you need

☐ 1 cup cold water

☐ 1 cup cornmeal

☐ 3 cups boiling water

☐ 1 teaspoon salt

☐ Flour

☐ Cooking oil

Directions

1. Mix the cold water with the cornmeal in a cooling pot.
2. Stir in the boiling water and salt. Cook over high heat, stirring constantly, until the mixture begins to boil.

3. Turn the heat to low and cover the pot. Let it cook for 10 minutes.

4. Pour the hot mush into a greased loaf pan. Cover it and chill it overnight.

5. Remove the cold mush from the pan. Slice it ½ inch thick. Coat each slice with flour. Fry it in oil until it is brown and crisp.

6. Eat it hot with butter or syrup.

Hominy

Hominy is a very fat, soft kernel of corn that tastes best when fried. It's made by soaking corn in lye to remove the hard hull. To emphasize that hominy is made of corn seeds, students can create a rebus chart that combines pictures with words for beginning readers. The children should draw a picture beside each ingredient or direction.

How to cook hominy

What you need

☐ Canned hominy

☐ 2 teaspoons butter

☐ Salt

☐ Pepper

Directions

1. Drain the liquid from the can.

2. Fry the hominy in butter.

3. Add salt and pepper.

4. Eat it while it's hot.

Hominy grits

Dried hominy is ground into a coarse cereal which is then cooked in water. It's often served in the South with other breakfast foods.

What you need

☐ 5 cups boiling water

☐ 1 teaspoon salt

☐ 1 cup grits

☐ Butter

Directions

1. Measure the water and salt into a pot. Bring the water to a boil.

2. Stir in the grits.

3. Cover the pot, reduce the heat, and let the grits cook for 25 minutes. Stir frequently to prevent the grits from sticking to the pot.

4. Eat it hot with salt and butter.

Rice recipes

Rice cereal

How many cereals containing rice can you find on the grocery store shelves? We found Rice Krispies®, Cream of Rice®, Rice Puffs®, and Rice Chex®, and we barely looked! Try Cream of Rice® hot cereal; follow cooking directions on the box.

Steamed rice

What you need

☐ A cooking pot with lid
☐ 2¼ cups water
☐ 1 cup rice
☐ Butter
☐ Salt
☐ Pepper

Directions

1. Measure the water into the cooking pot. Add the rice.
2. Cover the pot with a lid. Heat on high until the water begins to boil.
3. Stir the rice one time. Reduce the heat to low.
4. Cover the pot again. Let the rice cook for 25 minutes.
5. Add butter, salt, and pepper.

Fried rice

Cold left-over rice is delicious when it's fried!

What you need

☐ Vegetable cooking oil
☐ 2 eggs
☐ 1 stalk celery, diced
☐ 1 small onion, diced
☐ 2 cups cold cooked rice
☐ 1 tablespoon soy sauce

Directions

1. Pour a small amount of oil in a skillet. Add the eggs and scramble them with a fork. As soon as they are cooked, remove them from the skillet and set them aside.
2. Add a little more oil to the skillet. Fry the celery and onion until they are tender but not brown.
3. Add the rice, soy sauce, and cooked egg to the skillet. Mix everything together.
4. Cook the mixture slowly until it turns a golden brown on the bottom. Turn it over with a spatula, and let more of it turn golden brown.

Yield: 2½ cups fried rice

Rice pudding

This recipe uses rice that has been precooked, called instant rice. It makes a delicious dessert.

What you need
- ☐ 1 cup instant rice, uncooked
- ☐ 1½ cups milk
- ☐ ¼ cup sugar
- ☐ ¼ teaspoon salt
- ☐ ¼ teaspoon cinnamon

Directions
1. Mix the rice, milk, sugar, salt, and cinnamon in a saucepan. Cook it until it boils, stirring constantly.
2. Remove the pan from the heat. Cover it and let it stand 15 minutes.
3. Stir the pudding. Eat it hot. Try it with a little milk poured on top.

Yield: 2 cups

Oat recipes

Oat cereal

When we looked in the grocery store for breakfast cereals made from oats, we found oatmeal, Honey Nut Oatmeal Flakes®, Cheerios®, Oat Squares®, and granola. Honey Bunches of Oats® are made of oats, plus corn and wheat! How many oat cereals can you find on the grocery store shelves? Try cooking hot oatmeal cereal (porridge); follow the cooking directions on the box.

Chocolate chip oatmeal cookies

These cookies are a favorite of President Bill Clinton and his family.

What you need
- ☐ 1 cup solid shortening
- ☐ 1 cup brown sugar
- ☐ ½ cup granulated sugar
- ☐ 1 teaspoon vanilla extract
- ☐ 2 eggs
- ☐ 1½ cups all-purpose flour
- ☐ 1 teaspoon salt
- ☐ 1 teaspoon baking soda
- ☐ 2 cups old fashioned rolled oats
- ☐ 12-oz. package semisweet chocolate chips

Directions
1. Preheat the oven to 350°F.
2. Mix together the shortening, brown sugar, granulated sugar, vanilla, and eggs until creamy.

3. Add the flour, salt, and soda. Mix well.
4. Add the rolled oats. Mix well.
5. Stir in the chocolate chips.
6. Drop teaspoons of batter an inch apart onto a lightly-greased cookie sheet.
7. Bake 8 to 10 minutes until cookies are light brown.

Yield: 7 dozen cookies

Wheat recipes

Wheat cereal
There are lots of breakfast cereals made from wheat on the grocery store shelves. We found Bran Flakes®, Mini Wheats®, Clusters®, Raisin Bran®, Grape Nuts®, Cream of Wheat®, and Wheat Chex®. How many breakfast cereals containing wheat can you find? Cook hot wheat cereal (farina); buy Cream of Wheat® and follow the cooking directions on the box.

Pancakes
Pancakes were brought to America by Dutch settlers. They were baked in an open hearth in a long-handled pan, and were sometimes called hearth cakes.

What you need
☐ 1 egg
☐ 1¼ cups milk
☐ 2 tablespoons soft shortening
☐ 1¼ cups flour
☐ 1 teaspoon sugar
☐ 1½ teaspoons baking powder
☐ ½ teaspoon salt
☐ Butter
☐ Syrup

Directions
1. Mix together the egg, milk, shortening, flour, sugar, baking powder, and salt.
2. Pour the batter in pools a little apart on a hot griddle. If it is necessary, grease the griddle very lightly.
3. Turn the pancakes as soon as they are puffed and full of bubbles.
4. Serve them hot with butter and syrup.

Waffles
Early Dutch settlers brought waffle irons to America. They were long-handled and very hard to hold over a hot fire in the cooking hearth. The name means flat, honey-comb cakes. To make waffles you will need a waffle iron.

What you need

- ☐ 2 eggs
- ☐ 2 cups buttermilk
- ☐ 2 cups flour
- ☐ 2 teaspoons baking powder
- ☐ 1 teaspoon soda
- ☐ ½ teaspoon salt
- ☐ 6 tablespoons soft shortening

Directions

1. Heat the waffle iron while mixing the batter.
2. Mix together the eggs, buttermilk, flour, baking powder, soda, salt, and soft shortening until the batter is smooth.
3. Pour batter from a cup onto the hot waffle iron. Close the lid.
4. Cook until the steaming stops.
5. Lift the waffle off carefully with a fork. Eat it hot with butter and syrup.

Buttered macaroni

To emphasize that macaroni and other pasta are made of wheat seeds, students can create a rebus chart that combines pictures with words for beginning readers. The children should draw a picture beside each ingredient or direction.

What you need

- ☐ Saucepan
- ☐ 1 cup macaroni
- ☐ 1 tablespoon butter
- ☐ ¼ teaspoon salt

Directions

1. Bring a pot of water to a boil.
2. Add the macaroni.
3. Stir it to keep it from sticking.
4. Cook the macaroni 10 minutes until it is tender.
5. Drain the water.
6. Add butter and salt.
7. Eat it while it is hot!

Spaghetti with cheese

Spaghetti is made of wheat seeds. Sometimes spinach is added to make green spaghetti, and tomatoes are added to make red spaghetti.

What you need

- ☐ Spaghetti
- ☐ Butter
- ☐ Parmesan cheese, grated

Directions

1. Bring a pot of water to a boil.
2. Add spaghetti. Stir to keep it from sticking.
3. Cook the spaghetti 15 minutes, and then taste a piece. Continue cooking until it is tender.
4. Drain the water. Add butter and grated parmesan cheese.

Peanut recipes

Caution! Some children are extremely allergic to peanuts in any form. Before giving any kind of food to a child, be sure to get written approval from the child's parents.

Before making your own peanut butter, read the labels of several different commercial brands to see what is added to "store-bought" peanut butter.

How to make peanut butter

To emphasize that peanut butter is made of seeds of the peanut plant, students can create a rebus chart that combines pictures with words for beginning readers. The children should draw a picture beside each ingredient or direction.

What you need

☐ A 12-ounce bag of roasted, unsalted peanuts OR 1¾ cups shelled peanuts
☐ 1 teaspoon sugar
☐ ¼ teaspoon salt
☐ 3 tablespoons vegetable oil
☐ A food processor or blender
☐ Rubber spatula
☐ Plastic knife for each student
☐ Crackers

Directions

1. Shell the peanuts.
2. Remove the brown, papery membrane. It tastes bitter.
3. Pour the peanuts in the blender or food processor. Add the sugar, salt, and oil.
4. Process on HIGH until the peanuts have formed smooth, thick peanut butter. Stir with the rubber scraper when necessary.
5. Spread the peanut butter on toast. Hold a taste test to see if anyone can detect differences among several commercial brands of peanut butter and the peanut butter they have just made.

Peanut butter and jelly sandwiches

To emphasize that bread is made of wheat seeds, and peanut butter is made of seeds of the peanut plant, students can create a rebus chart that combines pictures with words for beginning readers. The children should draw a picture beside each ingredient or direction.

What you need

- ☐ 2 slices whole-wheat bread
- ☐ 1 tablespoon peanut butter
- ☐ 2 teaspoons jelly

Directions

1. Spread peanut butter on one slice of bread.
2. Spread jelly on another slice of bread.
3. Put them together to make a sandwich.
4. Eat half of the sandwich and share the rest with a friend.

Peanut butter cookies

Life without peanut butter cookies would be pretty dull. Thank goodness for seeds!

What you need

- ☐ 1 cup margarine (2 sticks)
- ☐ 1¼ cups brown sugar
- ☐ 1¼ cups white sugar
- ☐ 2 eggs
- ☐ 1 cup peanut butter
- ☐ 1¼ teaspoons vanilla extract
- ☐ 2½ cups flour
- ☐ 2 teaspoons baking powder
- ☐ 1¼ teaspoons baking soda
- ☐ ¼ teaspoon salt

Directions

1. Preheat the oven to 400°F.
2. Mix together the margarine, brown sugar, white sugar, eggs, peanut butter and vanilla until creamy.
3. Add the flour, baking powder, baking soda, and salt. Mix well.
4. Drop teaspoons of dough one inch apart on an ungreased baking sheet.
5. Flatten each cookie slightly with a fork dipped in flour. Press each cookie twice, making a crisscross design.
6. Bake at 400°F for about 10 minutes, until the cookies are light brown around the edges.

Bean recipes

Bean soup

Cook this delicious soup in a crock pot after the beans have soaked in water overnight. Eat it with crackers or cornmeal muffins.

What you need

- ☐ 16 oz. dry navy (small white) beans
- ☐ 7 cups cold water
- ☐ 2 stalks celery, chopped fine
- ☐ 2 carrots, chopped
- ☐ 1 large onion, minced
- ☐ 1 garlic clove, minced
- ☐ 2 teaspoons salt
- ☐ ¼ teaspoon pepper (a seed!)

Directions

1. Wash the dry beans under cold running water. Pour them into a crock pot and add the seven cups cold water. Cover the pot and let the beans soak overnight.
2. The next morning, add the celery, carrots, onion, garlic, salt, and pepper. Cook covered on high, stirring once in awhile to prevent the soup from burning on the bottom.
3. The soup should be ready to eat in about 3 hours, when the beans are tender.

Chili con carne

Chili recipes come to us from Mexico. The words con carne mean "with meat." This soup is made with ground beef.

What you need

- ☐ 1 lb. ground beef
- ☐ 1 large onion, chopped
- ☐ 1 clove garlic, minced
- ☐ 3 cups canned kidney beans, undrained
- ☐ 16 oz. can tomato sauce
- ☐ 3½ cups canned tomatoes
- ☐ 1 tablespoon chili powder
- ☐ 1 teaspoon sugar
- ☐ 2 teaspoons salt
- ☐ ½ teaspoon pepper
- ☐ 7 cups hot water

Directions

1. In a large saucepan, cook the ground beef until it loses its red color. Drain off the fat.
2. Add the rest of the ingredients. Cover the saucepan.
3. Simmer the soup for one hour, stirring occasionally.

Pea recipes

How to cook peas

Fresh peas from the garden or market are delicious seeds to eat. They can be cooked on a hot plate, on a stove, or in a microwave oven.

To emphasize that peas are seeds, students can create a rebus chart that combines pictures with words for beginning readers. The children should draw a picture beside each ingredient or direction.

What you need

☐ A cooking pot with a lid
☐ Canned, fresh, or frozen peas
☐ Butter

Directions

1. Put the peas in the cooking pot. Add a small amount of water to the pot to cook fresh or frozen peas.
2. Cook the peas until they are hot and tender. Most peas will cook in four minutes after the water comes to a boil.
3. Eat them hot with butter.

Split pea soup

Dried split peas have had the hull (outer covering) removed. They cook into a smooth green delicious soup. This recipe is perfect for a crock pot.

What you need

☐ 16 oz. dried split peas
☐ 6 cups water
☐ 2 potatoes, peeled and diced
☐ 1 large onion, chopped
☐ 2 stalks celery, chopped
☐ 2 carrots, chopped
☐ 1 clove garlic, minced
☐ 1 teaspoon salt
☐ ¼ teaspoon pepper

Directions

1. Rinse the dried peas under cold running water. Put them in the crock pot.
2. Add the remaining ingredients. (Refrigerate the entire crock pot overnight and cook the soup the next day, if you wish.)
3. Cover the crock pot and cook on high for about 6 hours, stirring once or twice, until the vegetables are tender and the soup is thick.
4. Eat it with crackers or buttered toast.

Cocoa bean recipes

Cocoa beans are roasted and then ground into a powder to make chocolate. The first chocolate drink was invented by a man in London, England in 1657. He called this wonderful new drink "jacolatte."

Hot chocolate

Hot chocolate made with unsweetened cocoa must be cooked in a saucepan, but the taste is worth the effort! To emphasize that chocolate foods are made of cocoa seeds, students can create a rebus chart that combines pictures with words for beginning readers. The children should draw a picture beside each ingredient or direction.

What you need

- ☐ ¼ cup sugar
- ☐ ¼ cup unsweetened cocoa
- ☐ 1 cup water
- ☐ 3 cups whole milk

Directions

1. Measure the sugar and cocoa into a saucepan. Mix them together.
2. Add the water. Cook over low heat, stirring constantly, until the mixture boils. Boil it one minute.
3. Stir in the whole milk. Heat it, but do not boil. Serve it hot.

Yield: Makes one quart of hot chocolate.

Chocolate waffle iron cookies

Use a waffle iron to make hot, fresh chocolate cookies.

What you need

- ☐ 1¼ cups sugar
- ☐ ½ cup solid shortening
- ☐ 2 eggs
- ☐ ½ cup milk
- ☐ 1½ cups flour
- ☐ ⅔ cup unsweetened cocoa
- ☐ 1 teaspoon baking powder
- ☐ ¼ teaspoon baking soda
- ☐ ½ teaspoon salt
- ☐ 1½ teaspoons vanilla
- ☐ No-stick cooking spray

Directions

1. Preheat the waffle iron on the "waffle" setting.
2. Mix together the sugar, shortening, and eggs. Stir in the milk.
3. Add the flour, cocoa, baking powder, baking soda, salt, and vanilla. Stir until smooth.

4. Spray the waffle iron with no-stick cooking spray.
5. Drop 1 teaspoon of dough on the hot waffle iron for each cookie. Close the lid and cook until the waffle iron light goes out, indicating that they are done (two or three minutes). Use a meat fork to lift the cookies from the iron.

Yield: 4 dozen cookies

chapter 2

Flowers

Science goals

To help children become aware of what flowers are and their usefulness to the world and our lives

Planning

If possible, plan to take a field trip to a local nursery so that the children can see many types of flowers. Children will enjoy seeing the flowers on cactus plants, the tremendous variety of beautiful roses, and/or many other fascinating kinds of flowers available in your area. If you cannot go there, see if someone from a nursery or florist can come talk to the children and bring flowers to see and discuss. Ask parents to bring flowers in to show or to donate flowers for the class to enjoy and study. Gather informational books from the library and have these available for the children.

Materials needed for discussion and activities

- ☐ Informational books
- ☐ Journals
- ☐ Pencils, crayons
- ☐ Live flowers
- ☐ Artificial flowers
- ☐ Easel, paints
- ☐ Construction paper
- ☐ Tools for planting flowers
- ☐ Play money
- ☐ Magnifying glasses

Related words

plants Living things that grow, but cannot move about like animals can, and usually produce their own food

When we say flower, we may mean an entire plant that has blossoms or we may mean just a blossom. Many plants have flowers, but often the flowers are so small or are not very colorful and we never notice them. Flowers grow all over the world, even in very cold areas. People enjoy flowers because of their colors and beauty.

☞ Activity idea: Flower journal

Science skills

Recording information

Before you begin your study, create a journal for each child to record information in. Sheets of plain white paper are best. You will need about 10 sheets. You will need a construction paper cover and back. It will probably be best to let the children make the cover after the journal is completed. It will stay in better shape, and the children will be able to use the knowledge they have acquired to show accuracy in their picture or writing. Here are some ideas for covers:

- ☐ Make photographs of each child doing something with flowers and glue a picture on that child's cover. Let the child write a sentence or dictate a sentence to you about the picture.
- ☐ Give children all colors of construction paper and let them cut and paste to create flowers for the cover.
- ☐ Provide magazines and let the children cut out pictures of flowers to glue onto the cover.
- ☐ Dry and press flowers by putting them between the pages of a phone book and laying something heavy on top for about two weeks. Lay the pressed flowers on the construction paper and laminate or cover with clear adhesive paper.
- ☐ Cut sponges into flower shapes and let children sponge paint flowers onto the cover. They can then add stems and leaves with green paint and a paintbrush or cotton swab.

💡 Discussion idea: Let's look at and talk about flowers

Science skills
Observing, asking questions

Provide a real plant, in a pot or outdoors, with flowers to show the children. Begin the observation by saying, "Look at this plant and tell me what you see." Let the children take turns getting very close to the plant and telling you something about the plant. Guide them in seeing the leaves, stems, roots (if possible), and flowers. Help them talk about colors. Let them feel of the plant and smell of the flowers. Let them discuss what they feel and smell. Talk about where the roots are.

Guide the children in looking at the flower. Show them the *sepals*, which are the leafy parts that protect the flower before it opens up. When the flower opens up, the sepals separate and the petals spread out. The sepals remain around the base of the flower or they curl back.

The *petals* are colorful parts of the flowers. Insects see the colors and are attracted to the flowers. Some flowers have many petals and some flowers have fewer petals.

Inside the petals are *stamens*. Their job is to make pollen. The top of a stamen has yellow pollen grains. Every flower has its own special pollen.

In the middle of the flower is a tube that leads to the seed case. This tube is called a *pistil*. The top of this tube is called the *stigma*. The stigma is sticky and it can catch pollen from other flowers that are the same kind. At the bottom of the pistil is the *ovary* where seeds develop.

Insects come to flowers for food. Some flowers produce nectar, which is a sweet liquid. Butterflies also like nectar. Bees come to flowers to collect pollen. Pollen grains stick to the insect's body. When the insect goes to another flower of the same type, some of those pollen grains may stick to the stigma, go on down to the seed case, and join with the seeds, and then the seeds can begin to grow. This is called *pollination*.

Let the children talk about why they like flowers and times they have given someone flowers or have received flowers. This might be a good time to talk about how flowers make us feel. People like to get flowers when they are sick or on a special occasion like a birthday. Flowers can make us feel very happy. We like to decorate with flowers during holidays and at weddings. Flowers look pretty and often smell good too, but they have a very important job. Their important job is to make seeds that will help new plants to grow. Flowers are brightly colored so that insects will see them and will be attracted to them.

After you have let the children carefully examine the flowers, talk about the rest of the plant.

The *stem* holds the leaves and flowers up so they can get sunlight. The stem is a special passageway for water and nutrients to travel from the roots. The stem also carries food from the leaves to other parts of the plant.

The leaves make food for the plant. Leaves are like little factories. They use sunlight, water, and carbon dioxide to make food. They also give off oxygen, which helps people and animals.

The roots give the plant support in the soil. The roots take in nutrients and water from the soil.

> ### Pollen Point
>
> *Flowering plants have four main parts: flowers, stems, leaves, and roots. They reproduce by growing seeds. Some flowers can reproduce without seeds. Bulbs, like the daffodil, have special parts which store food throughout the winter and so the plant is able to grow and reproduce the next year. Non-flowering plants do not have flowers. They reproduce by making spores. A spore is a single-cell reproductive organ. Fungi, mosses, ferns, and seaweed are examples of non-flowering plants.*

☞ Activity idea: Nature walk

Science skills
Observing, using numbers, asking questions, recording information

The children will need their journals, a clipboard to support their journal, a pencil, and crayons. Take a walk around your schoolyard or a nearby park at a time of the year when flowering plants are blooming. Whenever you find flowers, wild or garden flowers, let the children sit down and draw and color the flowers as accurately as possible. If you know the name of the flower, help the children write it. Let the children gently touch and smell the flowers if bees are not around and if it is safe to walk that close. Wildflowers may be surrounded by tall weeds that would not be safe to walk through.

Help the children notice whether each type of flower gets a lot of sun or very little sun. Some types of flowers need four or five hours of sunlight and other types of flowers like to be in the shade most of the time.

Talk with the children about the size of the flowers (how tall the plant is as well as how big the blossom is). If you have a ruler, measure the stems of the flowers and let the children record this information. Talk about the colors of the flowers. As you talk to the children use colors like: "soft pink," "bright yellow," "light blue," etc. Help children begin to notice shades of color.

Look for bees and butterflies around the flowers. The children may want to add these to their journals.

After about 30 minutes of these activities, return to the room and look through informational books to help identify any flowers that you did not know the names of. Let the children add these names to their pictures in the journals.

 ## Activity idea: Your favorite flower

 ### Science skills
Designing investigations, using numbers, drawing conclusions

Choose three pictures of flowers from a magazine or flower catalog. Tell the children that you want to let them choose their favorite flower of the three. Let the children help you decide on a way to let each child vote and how to record the results. Some possibilities are:

☐ Tape the pictures on the chalkboard. Let each child come to the board and put a checkmark below his favorite flower. After everyone has finished, add the checks and see which flower has the most.

☐ Glue the pictures on large pieces of construction paper. Let each child write his name on the piece of paper which has his favorite flower. When everyone has finished, add the number of names on each piece of paper.

☐ Make a graph. Glue the three pictures on the bottom of a large piece of paper. Draw columns with squares. Each child can color in one square to indicate his favorite flower. After everyone has finished, let the children look at the columns and tell you which one is the tallest. Now count the colored squares in each column to verify which has the most.

 ## Activity idea: Planting a flower garden

 ### Science skills
Following directions, classifying, manipulating materials, using numbers, applying knowledge

If it is possible, let the children plant their own flower garden, even if it is a very small one. Here are ideas for steps to follow:

1. Find a place outside for the garden. If possible choose a place near a water source so you can water the flowers easily.

2. Decide which kinds of plants will grow well in that location. Is it sunny or shady?

3. Send a note home asking parents to donate plants (or you may have already planted seeds which have sprouted and you can use these plants), topsoil, fertilizer, and tools that you will need. Also ask for help in planting.

4. Select a day when you have some parent volunteers to help and enjoy letting the children plant the flowers.

5. After the flowers have been planted, water them.

6. Talk to the children about how they will take care of the garden, specifically watering and pulling weeds up.

7. Let the children draw a picture of the garden in their journals and label the flowers.

 ## Activity idea: Enjoying poetry

 ## Science skills

Finding information, communicating information

Many poets have been inspired by the beauty of flowers. Get a collection of children's poetry books and look for poems about flowers. Read these to the children. Model for the children how you found the poems. (You may have looked at the illustrations, the title, or used the table of contents.) Afterwards, let the children look through the books for poems about flowers.

Activity idea: Writing poetry

Science skills

Observing, communicating information

Write a class poem. Provide a real flower for the children to look at, feel, and smell. Let each child contribute a word or phrase about the flower. Write these on the board. Then arrange the words and phrases into a logical sequence for a poem (poetry does not have to rhyme) on a piece of chart paper. Let the children think of a title for the poem. Read the finished poem to them several times until they can join in and read along also.

 ## Activity idea: Examining flowers

Science skills

Observing, recording information, using numbers, manipulating materials

Give children opportunities to look closely at real flowers and record information in their journals. Cut flowers in a vase or flowers in a pot are wonderful. These could be placed on a large table and individual children can sit beside the flower while they draw and color it in their journal. Write the name of each flower on a card and place the card beside the flower. The children can use magnifying glasses to help them learn more about the flowers. Encourage and model gentleness so that children will not harm the plants in any way.

Pollen Point

You can create dried water colors from liquid tempera. You will need liquid tempera in several colors and empty margarine tubs or other such containers. Fill each container ¾ full of liquid tempera paint. Let the paint sit uncovered until it completely dries out. This may take several weeks. The children can now dip their brushes in water and then onto the hardened tempera. There will be no worry about spilled paint.

Activity idea: A book of flowers to color

 Science skills

Recording information

A book of flowers to color is provided to be duplicated for each child. You can cut each large page in half and then staple all of the pages together to make a book. Help the children read about these flowers and look at pictures in encyclopedias and other reference materials.

See Figs. 2-1, 2-2, 2-3, 2-4, 2-5, and 2-6 for the pages to include in the flower book.

Let's create a paper plate sunflower

It's often said that the sunflower follows the path of the sun across the sky by slowly turning its head. Some sunflowers grow to be twelve feet tall! (See Fig. 2-7 for a sample paper plate sunflower.)

 Science skills

Observing a real sunflower, creating a sunflower model, following directions, manipulating materials

What you need

- [ ] A real sunflower, or colored pictures of them
- [ ] A 9-inch white paper plate
- [ ] Crayons
- [ ] Yellow and green construction paper
- [ ] Scissors
- [ ] White glue
- [ ] Sunflower seeds (bird seed)
- [ ] Shelled, salted sunflower seeds (Sold in grocery stores as a snack food.)

Directions

1. Examine a real sunflower or look at pictures of sunflowers. Color the paper plate to make it look like the center of a real flower. It might be brown, yellow, or even purple.

2. Use the sunflower ray pattern in Fig. 2-8 to trace and cut out 20 rays (petals) from yellow paper.
3. Glue the rays on the plate.
4. Cut a long stem from green paper. Use the leaf pattern in Fig. 2-8 to trace and cut out two or three leaves. Glue the leaves on the stem, and glue the stem on the bottom of the sunflower.
5. Glue sunflower seeds (bird seed) in the center of the flower. Let the glue dry, and then display your sunflower on a bulletin board or wall.
6. A second way to use this project is to turn it into a *wildlife feeder*. Construct the plate as above, but do not add the stem and leaves. Instead of gluing seeds to the middle of the plate, pile sunflower seeds on the plate, and put it outside on a table, tree stump, or bench for birds and squirrels to find.

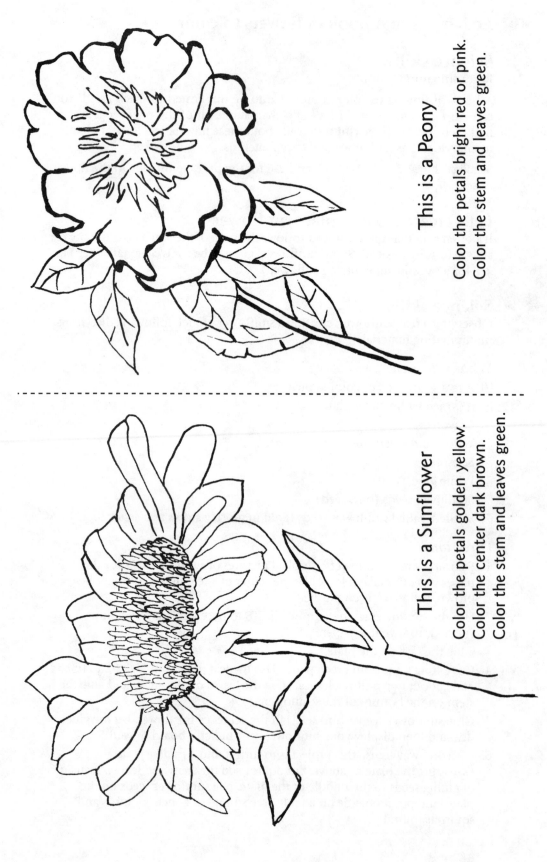

This is a Peony

Color the petals bright red or pink.
Color the stem and leaves green.

■ **2-2** *A peony.*

This is a Sunflower

Color the petals golden yellow.
Color the center dark brown.
Color the stem and leaves green.

■ **2-1** *A sunflower.*

These are Pansies

Color the petals blue, purple, or yellow.

■ **2-4** *Pansies.*

This is a Daffodil

Color it yellow.
Color the stem and leaves green.

■ **2-3** *A daffodil.*

49

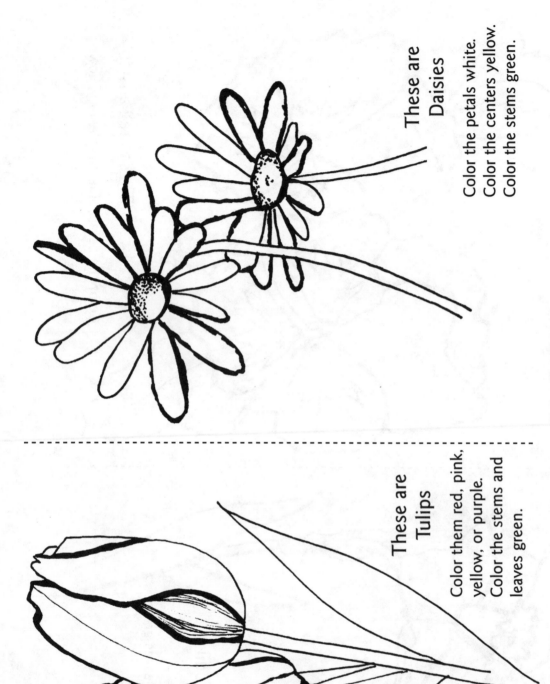

These are
Daisies

Color the petals white.
Color the centers yellow.
Color the stems green.

■ **2-6** *Some Daisies.*

These are
Tulips

Color them red, pink,
yellow, or purple.
Color the stems and
leaves green.

■ **2-5** *Some Tulips.*

■ **2-7** *A paper plate sunflower.*

7. A third way to use this project is to turn it into a *sunflower serving plate*. Construct the plate as above, but do not color it or add the stem and leaves. Fill the center of the sunflower with shelled, salted sunflower seeds for a bright and healthy snack.

Let's create a tissue paper peony

Peonies bloom in late spring. The large ruffled flowers come in hues of red, pink, white, and have a wonderful fragrance.

 ### Science skills

Observing a real peony, creating a model, following directions, manipulating materials

What you need

☐ A real peony, or colored pictures of them (Look in flower catalogs for pictures.)

☐ 4 sheets of tissue wrapping paper, 1 foot 6 inches × 2 feet 2 inches

☐ Scissors

☐ Small rubber band

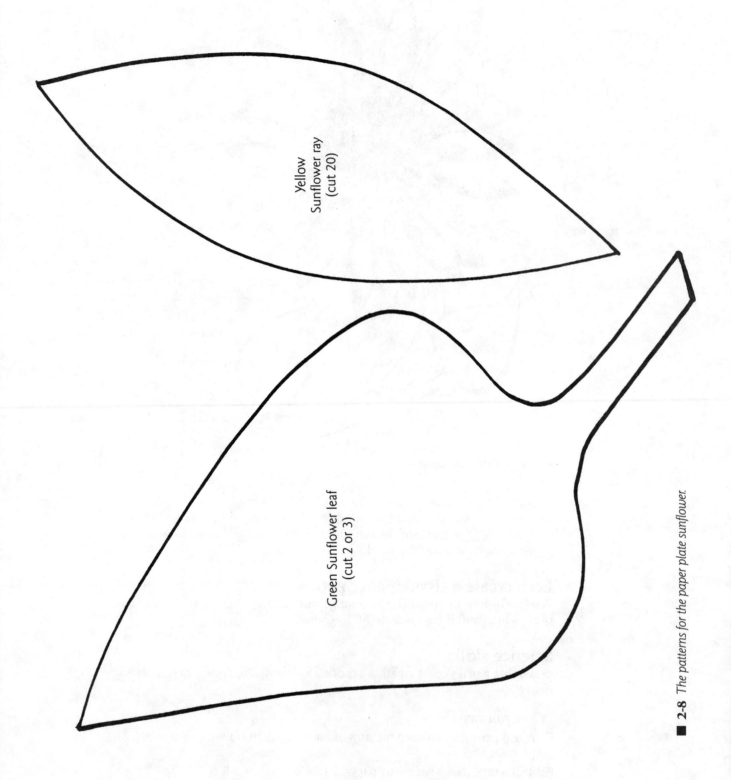

Yellow
Sunflower ray
(cut 20)

Green Sunflower leaf
(cut 2 or 3)

■ **2-8** *The patterns for the paper plate sunflower.*

Directions

1. Cut each sheet of tissue paper in half.
2. Stack the sheets on top of each other, and treat them as if they are a single sheet.
3. Start at the narrow end of the sheets, and fold them in ½-inch pleats. Press down hard to crease the folded edges.
4. Double a rubber band tightly around the middle of the pleated tissue (see Fig. 2-9).

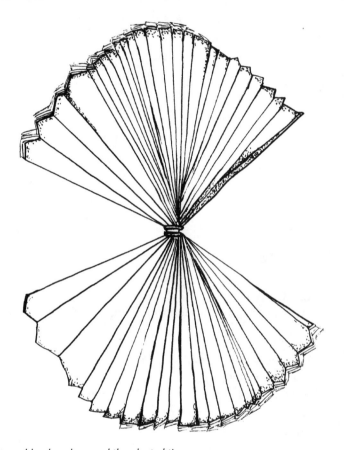

■ **2-9** *Put a rubber band around the pleated tissue.*

5. Carefully separate one sheet of tissue paper. Tug at it gently until it is sticking up in the air. Continue pulling it upward completely around the flower.
6. Repeat this step with each tissue paper layer until all the layers are pulled up.
7. Pull the bottom layer downward all the way around to give the peony a fluffy look.

Let's create a daffodil
A foam egg carton can be turned into a bouquet of daffodils. (See Fig. 2-10.)

■ **2-10** *An egg carton daffodil.*

Science skills
Observing, creating a model, following directions, manipulating materials

What you need
☐ Daffodils or photographs of daffodils (The children can look in gardening catalogs.)
☐ Styrofoam egg carton
☐ Yellow construction paper
☐ Pencil
☐ Green pipe cleaners
☐ Scissors

Directions
1. Cut the lid off the egg carton and discard it. Cut the carton into 12 separate eggcups.
2. Trim the sides of each cup so that it looks like the center of a daffodil.
3. Use the pattern in Fig. 2-11 to trace 12 petal shapes on yellow construction paper. Cut them out.
4. Use a pencil to poke a hole in the middle of each petal shape and each eggcup.
5. To make a daffodil model, thread a pipe cleaner through a petal shape and then through an egg cup.

Daffodil
petal
shape

 2-11 *The pattern for the daffodil.*

6. Bend the tip of the pipe cleaner over on the inside of the eggcup to hold it in place. Make a second little bend under the petal shape to keep it from sliding down the stem.

Let's create a pansy
Figure 2-12 shows the pansy you can create.

Pansies are cool weather bloomers which makes them perfect for spring or fall planting. In warm areas of the United States pansies are planted in the fall and bloom all winter!

Science skills
Observing, creating a model, following directions, manipulating materials

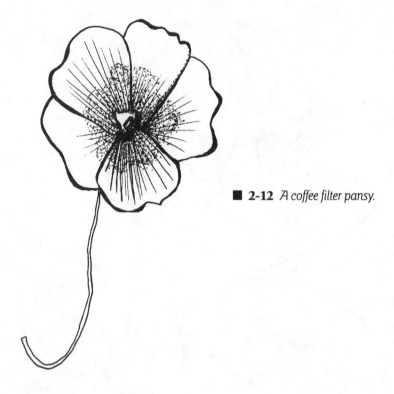

■ **2-12** *A coffee filter pansy.*

What you need
- ☐ Pansies or photographs of pansies
- ☐ Coffee filters
- ☐ Green construction paper
- ☐ Markers or water colors
- ☐ Scissors
- ☐ Pencil
- ☐ Green pipe cleaners

Directions
1. Look at some pansies or at pictures of pansies. They have five petals and yellow centers.
2. Use the patterns in Fig. 2-13 to trace and cut out five pansy petals from coffee filters. Cut out a green construction paper base. Make a tiny hole in the base and in each petal as shown on the pattern.
3. Color each of the coffee filter petals with markers or with water colors. Try to make them look like real pansy petals. The narrow end of each petal should be colored yellow, for instance.
4. Thread the base onto a pipe cleaner. Thread the five petals on top of the base. Turn the petals so they are in the same position as the petals of a real pansy.

Let's create a tulip
Figure 2-14 shows the construction paper tulip you can make.

Tulips grow in such a wide range of colors that your model can be any color you choose!

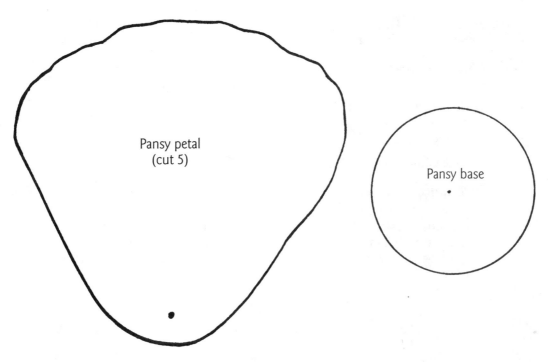

■ **2-13** *The patterns for the pansy petals and base.*

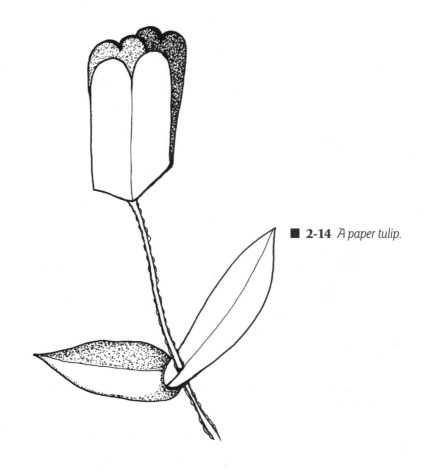

■ **2-14** *A paper tulip.*

Science skills
Observing, creating a model, following directions, manipulating materials

What you need
☐ Tulips or photographs of tulips (Look in gardening catalogs.)
☐ Construction paper in many colors
☐ Scissors
☐ Pencil
☐ Green pipe cleaners

Directions
1. Choose tulip colors that are your favorites; then try to copy them with construction paper. Use the patterns in Fig. 2-15 to trace and cut out three tulip petal shapes and two green tulip leaves from construction paper. Use a pencil to poke tiny holes in the petals and leaves as shown on the pattern.

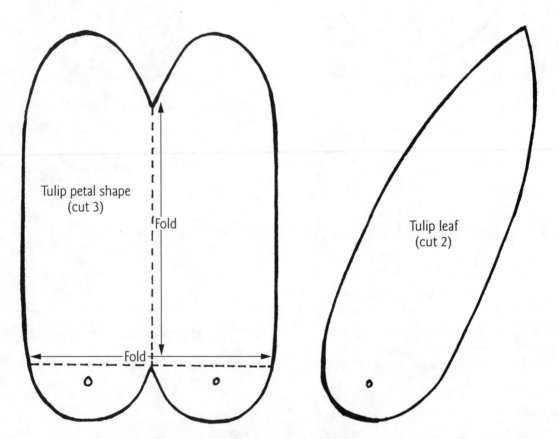

Tulip petal shape
(cut 3)

Fold

Fold

Tulip leaf
(cut 2)

■ **2-15** *The patterns for the tulip petal and leaf.*

2. Fold each petal shape in half as shown on the pattern. Fold up the bottom as shown on the pattern.

3. Thread a pipe cleaner through two leaves. Overlap the folded bottoms of one tulip petal shape so that their holes line up. Thread the pipe cleaner through the underside of the overlaps, as shown in Fig. 2-16.

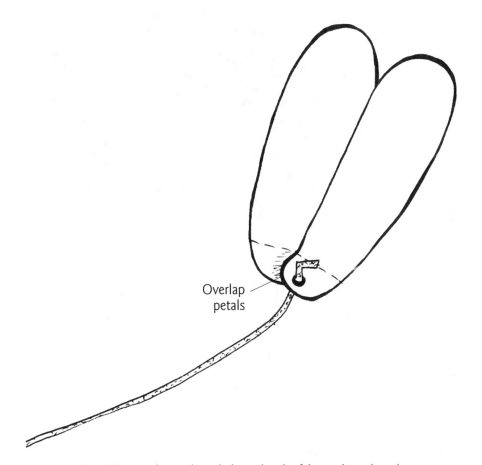

Overlap
petals

■ **2-16** *Thread the pipe cleaner through the underside of the overlapped petals.*

4. Add the remaining two tulip petal shapes, threading them one at a time down the pipe cleaner stem. Turn the petal shapes so they form a six-petal tulip.

Let's create a daisy
First examine a real daisy. Then create a paper model (see Fig. 2-17).

Science skills
Observing, creating a model, following directions, manipulating materials

What you need
☐ Daisies or photographs of daisies (The children can look in gardening catalogs.)
☐ Green, white, and yellow construction paper
☐ Green tissue paper

■ **2-17** *Paper daisies.*

☐ Pencil
☐ Green pipe cleaners
☐ Scissors

✂ *Directions*

1. Use the patterns in Fig. 2-18 to trace and cut out the following shapes from construction paper: white daisy rays, yellow centers, and green base. Cut the daisy leaves from green tissue paper. Cut a slit in the leaves as shown on the pattern.

2. Make a tiny hole with a pencil in the middle of each ray, center, and base, as shown on the pattern.

3. Thread a pipe cleaner first through the green base, then through the white rays, and last through the yellow center.

4. Curl the petals of the green base downward by pressing them around the pencil. Curl the white daisy rays up slightly.

5. To finish the model, lay the pipe cleaner stem in the middle of the tissue paper leaves. Bring one end of the leaf up and over the pipe cleaner, and insert that leaf in the slit. Pull the leaf through. Tug the leaves gently (don't rip the tissue paper) until they fit snugly on the pipe cleaner stem, one on each side.

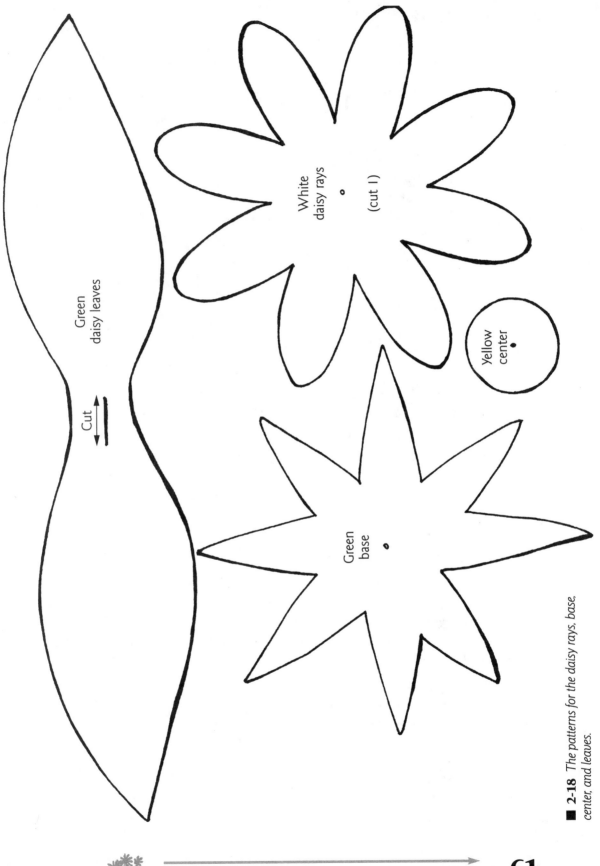

Green
daisy leaves

Cut

White
daisy rays

(cut 1)

Yellow
center

Green
base

■ **2-18** *The patterns for the daisy rays, base, center, and leaves.*

Let's create a flower and leaf bookmark

Small leaves and flowers can be preserved as a fascinating bookmark (see Fig. 2-19) to use or to give as a gift.

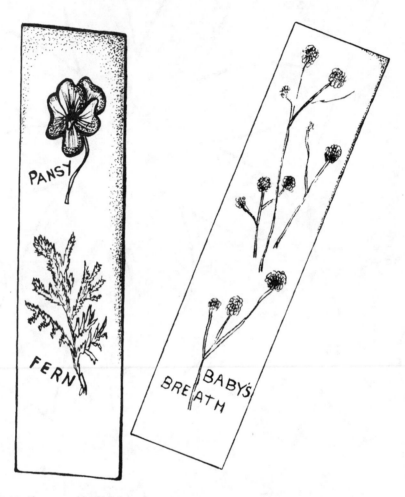

■ **2-19** *Flower and leaf bookmarks.*

 ## Science skills

Observing, finding and communicating information, following directions, manipulating materials

What you need

- ☐ Small leaves and tiny flowers
- ☐ Leaf and flower reference books to identify your samples
- ☐ A heavy telephone book (or use coffee filters)
- ☐ Ruler
- ☐ Construction paper
- ☐ Scissors

☐ White glue

☐ Clear Contact paper

Directions

1. Try to identify the leaves and flowers you have collected.

2. Arrange them single layer between the pages of a heavy telephone book, or sandwich them between two flattened coffee filters, and place a heavy book on top. Let them dry undisturbed for a week.

3. Use the ruler to measure construction paper rectangles 1½ × 7 inches. Cut out a rectangle for each bookmark you wish to make.

4. Glue the dried leaves and flowers on the construction paper in a single layer. Write the name of each one under it. Let the glue dry until it is hard and clear.

5. Sandwich the bookmarks between two pieces of clear Contact paper. Rub them carefully to eliminate air bubbles.

6. Trim the extra Contact paper from the edges of each bookmark.

Activity idea: A bulletin board of flowers to measure

Science skills

Following directions, creating models, measuring, using numbers, recording information

The purpose of this activity is for each child to make a flower in a pot that all of the children can measure. The completed flowers and the pots will need to be about 10 to 15 inches (inclusive of everything). You will need to provide pictures of real flowers and actual flowers for the children to observe as they create that certain type of flower. Each child will need brown construction paper to make a pot for his flower. Each child should put his name on the front of the pot so that it can be easily read.

Each child will need green construction paper to make a stem and leaves and various colors of paper to make the flower. Encourage the children to make the leaves just like the leaves of the real flower, etc. Help the children as they make their flowers and then let them glue the stem onto the back of the pot. You will need to staple each completed project onto a large bulletin board.

When you are ready to let the children measure, provide each child with a piece of paper with all of the children's names and two lines out beside for inches, and "centimeters." The children will need an inch ruler and a centimeter ruler. Three or four children at a time can come to the bulletin board and measure the height of the stem and flower (total of both) and record their information beside the correct child's name.

Activity idea: Make a big book

Science skills

Observing, finding information, recording information

Get large pieces of white construction paper or poster board (about 18 inches by 11 inches). Prepare the easel or a large table with containers of paint and large paint brushes. Have real flowers, artificial flowers, and pictures (in informational books) available. Ask each child to choose one type of flower to paint on the paper. Let each child paint a large flower and then write or you can write, the name of the flower below it. When all of the pictures are painted and have dried, bind them into a big book. When you present the book to the class, open each page and let the child who painted that picture come stand beside it and read the name. During subsequent readings let all of the children try to say or read the names of the flowers.

 ## Activity idea: Flower wall mural

 ## Science skills

Observing, classifying, finding information, communicating information, applying knowledge

Get a piece of light blue craft paper about six feet long and about three feet wide. Secure this to the wall. This will be the background. Now glue on a piece of green (all the way across, but not as wide) for grass. Cut the green so that it is curvy on the top. You might want to add a sun.

Now provide the children with many different colors of construction paper and informational books about flowers as well as real flowers to observe. Let the children make paper flowers for the mural. They should be encouraged to make each flower as realistic as possible in terms of shape of petals, colors, and shape of leaves. If several children make a certain kind of flower, let them place like kinds of flowers together on the mural. They can glue their completed flowers on the mural and then you or they need to label each kind of flower. You may want to use strips of white construction paper and colored markers to write the names. The finished mural will be beautiful and very educational, and all who view it will learn something about flowers.

Activity idea: Closure

Science skills

Classifying, creating models, using numbers, finding information, recording information, applying knowledge

A wonderful way to incorporate all of what the children have learned and done would be to create a "Flower Shop." This shop will be a place where people can come to look at flowers, learn about flowers, and buy flowers. Ask the children to bring in artificial flowers, real flowers in plastic pots, and pictures of flowers. Get play money, old checks, and old credit cards for the children to use for their purchases. Set aside an area of the room for the shop. Guide the children in putting the flowers in groups, according to kind, color, container, or by price.

Let the children name their shop and make signs for the shop. Let them price items. Get a play cash register, a telephone, and paper for receipts. Put the informational books about flowers in a certain area of the shop. The children can pretend to purchase these.

Have a schedule posted so that each day certain children will get to take various roles, such as sales clerk, stock person, craft person (who makes items to sell in the shop), and visitor guide (who takes visitors to see the flower garden, shows them around the shop, and also teaches the visitors about flowers).

The models that the children have created throughout the study will be perfect items for the store also. The children will have so much fun preparing and working in this "Flower Shop."

The Flower Cookbook

Although we eat large numbers of seeds prepared in many ways, we don't eat very many flowers. Two common edible flowers are cauliflower and broccoli.

Steamed cauliflower with cheese
Cauliflower with cheese is full of golden flavor.

What you will need
☐ Fresh cauliflower
☐ Salt
☐ Processed cheddar cheese slices
☐ Paprika

Directions
1. Remove the leaves from the cauliflower. Wash it under running water.
2. Place the cauliflower in a saucepan. Add two inches of water and a pinch of salt.
3. Cover the saucepan and bring the water to a boil. Reduce the heat. Cook the cauliflower until it can be easily pierced with a meat fork. Drain the cooking water.
4. Cover the cauliflower with several slices of processed cheddar cheese. Sift on some paprika. Put the lid back on the saucepan until the cheese melts. Serve it hot.

How to make broccoli with cottage cheese dip
Fresh broccoli is tasty when served with a creamy dip made with a blender or food processor. To emphasize that broccoli is a flower, students can create a rebus chart that combines pictures with words for beginning readers. The children should draw a picture beside each ingredient or direction.

What you will need
☐ Fresh broccoli
☐ 2 cups small curd cottage cheese
☐ ½ cup mayonnaise
☐ ⅛ teaspoon garlic powder
☐ ¼ teaspoon onion salt
☐ Pinch of freshly ground black pepper
☐ ⅛ teaspoon chili powder
☐ ¼ cup whole milk

Directions
1. Wash the broccoli in cold running water. Cut it into bite-sized florets.
2. To make the dip, add the cottage cheese, mayonnaise, garlic powder, onion salt, pepper, and chili powder to a blender or food processor.
3. Process on high for a few seconds until the dip is smooth. Add the milk and process again for a few seconds.
4. Pour the dip into individual bowls for dipping.

chapter 3

Trees

Science goals

To help children become more aware of trees in their environment and their usefulness to our lives

Planning

You need to do two very important things in this study of trees. One, you need to plant a young tree, so that the children can see how to plant a tree, how to care for a tree, and how to experience its growth. This process of nurturing is critical if children are to develop a real sense of loving and feeling responsible for nature. You may want to ask parents to help with this project. Two, you need to adopt a tree somewhere in the area, to observe over a long period of time. A big tree (more than 15 feet tall) would be preferable. Look for these two sections in this chapter: "Planting Your Own Tree," and "Adopting A Tree."

Gather informational books about trees and leaves. Gather magazines that would have pictures of trees. Have all of these available for children's use.

Get a camera and film for making pictures of trees throughout the seasons.

Materials needed for discussion and activities

- ☐ Informational books
- ☐ Journals
- ☐ Pencils, crayons
- ☐ Construction paper
- ☐ Camera
- ☐ Tools and materials for planting a tree
- ☐ Waxed paper
- ☐ An iron

Related words

plants Living things that grow, but cannot move about like animals can, and usually produce their own food

minerals Nonliving materials in soil that help a plant grow (examples are: potassium, calcium, nitrogen, iron)

What is a tree? Trees are plants that grow to be tall, at least 15 feet tall when they are fully grown. Trees can live for a long time. Some live for hundreds and some live for thousands of years. Did you know that there were trees on earth when dinosaurs lived?

Trees usually have one trunk which is protected by bark. Trees have branches. Trees have leaves. Trees have roots which go down into the ground. Trees may have flowers, fruit, or seeds.

The part of the tree with the leaves is called the *crown*. The crown includes branches, leaves, buds, flowers, and/or fruit. The shapes of crowns are interesting. Some are shaped like circles, ovals, triangles, and other interesting shapes.

Activity idea: Create a journal

Science skills

Recording information

Before you begin your study, create a journal for each child to record information in. Sheets of plain white paper are best. Decide on the number of sheets you need, but perhaps about 10 would be fine. You will need a construction paper front and back. Follow the directions for "Let's Create Whooo Needs A Tree?" to make a cover for the journal.

Let's create a tree-things picture

Go for a walk in the woods or park and collect things that have fallen from trees. Mount them in a special frame. (See Fig. 3-1 for a finished picture.)

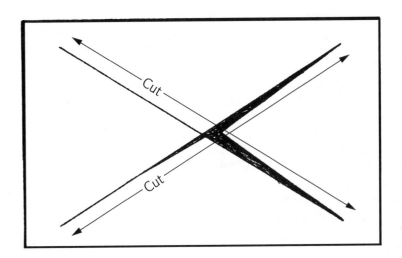

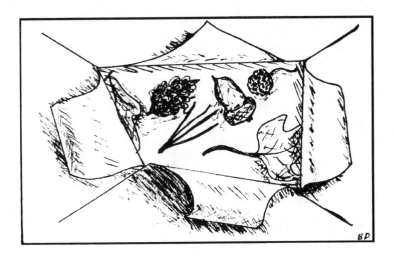

■ **3-1** *How to make a tree-things picture.*

Science skills

Observing, categorizing, finding information, following directions, manipulating materials

What you need
- [ ] A book that identifies trees
- [ ] Construction paper
- [ ] Pencil
- [ ] Ruler
- [ ] Scissors
- [ ] Glue
- [ ] Tube of clear, household cement

Directions

1. Go outside and gather tree things from the ground. Your tree things might include a leaf, a small pine cone, an acorn or other seed, pod, or flower. Use reference material to identify the tree they might have come from. Set them aside while you create a frame.

2. Use a pencil and ruler to draw a large X corner-to-corner on one sheet of construction paper. Cut on the X lines. The cuts form four triangles in the center of the paper.

3. Starting at the tip, roll one of the triangles around the pencil to curl it. Remove the pencil and the curl will remain. Repeat with the remaining triangles until all four are curled away from the center of the paper.

4. Turn the paper over. Spread glue around its edges. Carefully glue it on top of a second sheet of construction paper.

5. Glue some of your tree things inside the curled frame, using clear, household cement. Write the name of the tree or trees on the outside of the frame. Lay it flat to dry overnight.

Let's create "Whooo needs a tree?"

Many birds and animals rely on trees for a home. With this project you can show whooo needs a tree. (See Fig. 3-2.)

Science skills

Finding and communicating information, following directions, creating a model, manipulating materials

What you need
- [ ] White construction paper
- [ ] Scissors
- [ ] Glue
- [ ] Markers or crayons
- [ ] Nature magazines (optional)

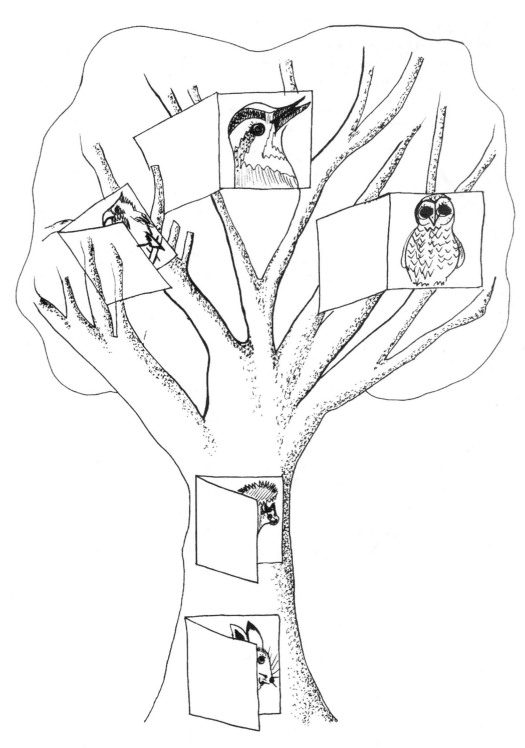

■ **3-2** *"Whooo needs a tree?"*

Directions

1. Use the pattern in Fig. 3-3 to trace the tree shape onto one sheet of white construction paper. Color it with markers or crayons. Be sure to add branches for wildlife to sit on.

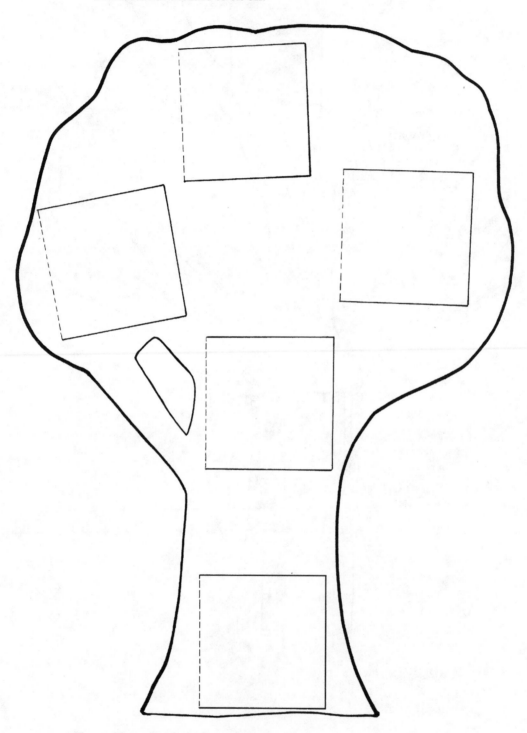

■ **3-3** *The pattern for "Whooo needs a tree?"*

2. Trace around the five windows. Cut out three sides of each window so that it opens.

3. Lay this drawing on a second sheet of paper the same size. Glue the drawing to the second sheet, being careful to leave each window open.

4. Inside each window, glue a picture of an animal that needs the tree for a home. We chose a rabbit, squirrel, woodpecker, cardinal, and owl. You might want to add tree frogs, crickets, moths, beetles, bees, and any number of other forest dwellers.

5. Close the windows when the glue has dried, then ask your family to guess whooo needs a tree?!

 ## Activity idea: Nature walk

Science skills
Observing, asking questions

Take the children outside to look at trees. Let them take their journals, pencils, and/or crayons.

As you take your walk, point out plants that are not trees, as well as plants that are trees. You might want to play a game called "Is This A Tree?" Point to a plant or object and ask the children "Is this a tree?" They should answer "yes" or "no" and then tell you why they gave that answer. For example, you might point to a blade of grass and ask, "Is this a tree?" The children will probably say "no." They then can tell you that the answer is no because the grass is very short, it does not have a trunk or stems or leaves.

As you point to trees and the children say "yes," spend time talking about and looking at the trunk (What color is it? How does it feel?), the branches, the leaves (What color are they? What shape are they? How do they feel?), and the roots (Can you see any of the roots?). Talk about how tall each tree is. Be sure to point out young trees (seedlings) that may be only one to five feet tall. Help the children understand that these are baby trees that will grow much taller as they get older. Talk about the shape of the crown of each tree.

Tell the children that trees provide homes for many animals like birds, squirrels, raccoons, and insects. Help the children look for nests or animals in trees.

Help the children record the date on a page of their journal and then let them write or draw information from this nature walk.

A tree is made up of different parts. Each part is very important. The trunk of the tree holds the tree up and supports the branches and leaves. The trunk of the tree contains tubes that carry water, minerals, and food up and down the tree. The trunk is protected by a tough outer layer called the *bark*. The bark protects the inside of the trunk from too much heat or cold. The bark keep insects out. Sometimes you can find out the name of a tree by looking at the bark.

Each year a tree grows thicker and taller. The trunks gets wider and taller so it can support the weight of branches as they are growing also. If we could look inside the trunk, we would see rings. We could count the rings to see how many years old the tree is. Two rings would mean two years old. You can also tell something about the weather during each year by looking at individual rings. Wide rings indicate plenty of rain and narrow rings indicate dry weather.

Branches grow out from the trunk. Branches give a tree its shape and support leaves.

Leaves make food for trees. This process is called *photosynthesis*. Leaves take in sunlight and use the sunlight, water from the soil, and carbon dioxide (a gas from the air) to make food for the entire tree. The tree could not live without this food. This food is stored not only in the roots and leaves of trees but also in fruits and seeds of trees. People eat the fruits and seeds. Animals eat fruits, seeds, and leaves of trees. During photosynthesis, oxygen is released by the leaves. People and animals need oxygen to breathe in order to live.

Pollen Point

Chlorophyll absorbs light energy from the sun and changes it into chemical energy which the tree is able to use.

Leaves have three main parts. The flat part around the veins is the *blade*. This part of the leaf has many green cells that help make food for the tree. The stem is called a *petiole*. The lines in leaves are called *veins*. Veins carry food and water. They also support the blade of the leaf.

Leaves have many different shapes. You can often identify a tree by looking at its leaves. Some leaves have smooth edges, and some have jagged edges. Some leaves are very broad and flat. Some leaves are very thin and needle-like.

Some trees have leaves that stay green all the time. These trees do not lose their leaves in the fall. These trees are called *evergreens*. Some trees have leaves that change color in the fall. Leaves may turn yellow, orange, red, purple, or brown. These colors were always there but were hidden by the green chlorophyll. Chlorophyll is an important substance in leaves that helps the leaves use sunlight to make food. In autumn, the days get shorter and there is less daylight. When there is less daylight, the leaves cannot make as much food. Less chlorphyll is made. The green coloring of the leaf goes away and then we see the leaf's secret colors. The leaves soon fall off because no more food is being made. The leaves fall to the ground and provide nutrients for the soil. The tree is able to rest during the winter. In the spring, the days will become warmer and there will be longer periods of sunlight. Food that has been stored in the roots will come up through the branches and help new leaves to grow.

Let's create a crown of fresh fall leaves
Become King or Queen of the forest as you learn more about trees. (See Fig. 3-4 for a picture of the crown.)

 ## Science skills
Observing, following directions, manipulating materials, classifying, finding and communicating information

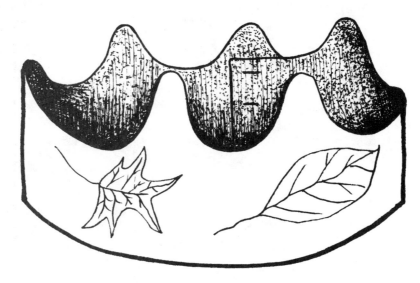

■ **3-4** *The crown of fresh fall leaves.*

What you need
☐ A place to gather leaves
☐ A tree identification book
☐ Poster paper
☐ Scissors
☐ Stapler
☐ Markers
☐ Glue

Directions

1. Collect some fall leaves. Identify each one by using a tree identification book.
2. Each crown is made of a piece of poster paper 6 × 24 inches. Cut out the pattern in Fig. 3-5.
3. Lay the pattern on the poster paper. Trace around the pattern, move it over, trace around it again, repeating until the entire piece of poster paper is drawn with the crown shape. Cut it out.
4. Decorate the crown with markers. Have someone help you fit the crown around your head and staple it into a circle.
5. Glue leaves around the outside of the crown. Write the name of each leaf on the crown.

Let's create ironed leaves in wax paper
Let's go for a walk and gather leaves for this project (shown in Fig. 3-6). Name the leaves by looking them up in a tree book.

Science skills
Observing, following directions, manipulating materials, classifying, finding and communicating information

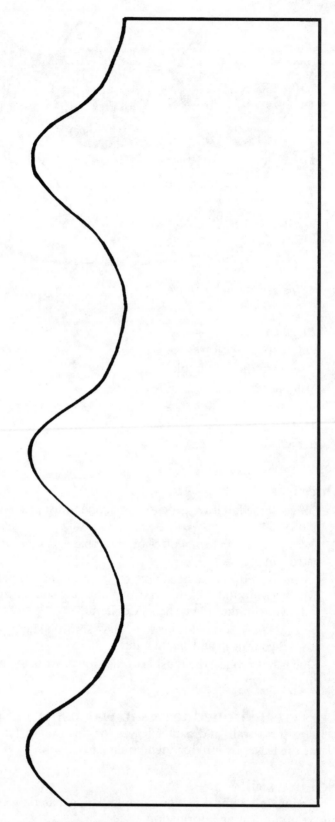

■ **3-5** *The pattern for "Let's create a crown."*

■ **3-6** *Fall leaves in wax paper.*

What you need

- ☐ A place to gather leaves
- ☐ A tree identification book
- ☐ Padded ironing board
- ☐ Iron
- ☐ Newspaper
- ☐ Wax paper
- ☐ File folder
- ☐ Tape

Directions

1. After you have gathered some leaves, choose two or three that are fairly flat and not too dry to identify and iron.
2. Adjust the ironing board so it is low enough to reach easily. Use a dry iron and turn the temperature gauge to the low setting. Put two layers of newspaper on the ironing board.
3. Each person will need a 16-inch piece of wax paper. Fold the wax paper in half like a book and place it on the newspaper layers.
4. Open the wax paper "book" and arrange your leaves on half of it, single layer. Close the "book" so the leaves are sandwiched in the wax paper. Lay a single sheet of newspaper on top of the wax paper.

 5. For Adults: Each child can iron her newspaper while you hold both of her hands. Put one hand over her hand as she glides the iron over the paper; hold her other hand away from the hot iron. Children automatically try to involve both hands in their work. Hold both hands so they don't get burned.

6. Lift the top newspaper. Gently remove the wax paper with the leaves sealed inside. Let it cool a few minutes.

7. Cut the center from both sides of a file folder to make a frame. Trim the extra wax paper from around your leaves, and tape them inside the file folder frame.

8. Write the names of your leaves on the outside of the frame.

Let's create leaf-print eggs
It's fun to dye eggs with a leaf silhouette. (See Fig. 3-7.)

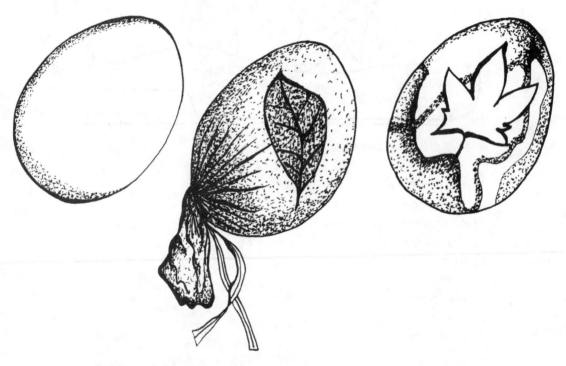

■ **3-7** *Let's create leaf-print eggs.*

🔍 Science skills
Observing the differences among leaves, finding and communicating information, following directions, manipulating materials

What you need
☐ One small, fresh leaf from a tree
☐ One hard-cooked egg per child
☐ Crayon
☐ A nylon stocking
☐ Liquid food color
☐ Vinegar
☐ Small bowls for dipping eggs in color
☐ Plastic spoons for dipping eggs
☐ Paper towels
☐ Newspapers to cover tables

Directions

1. Identify your leaf, using reference material if necessary.
2. Write the name of the leaf on a hard-cooked egg with a crayon. Put the leaf on the egg. Hold it in place by putting the egg inside a nylon stocking and securing the stocking with a twist tie.
3. Follow the directions on a box of food color to mix four cups of color: red, yellow, blue, and green, except use cool water instead of boiling water.
4. Dip the egg in the food dye. Let it dry on paper towels, or hang it to drip dry on an outdoor clothesline.
5. Remove the nylon and the leaf. A white silhouette of the leaf and the leaf's name will show on the egg.

Let's create a three-cone evergreen tree

Three cones stacked together make a beautiful evergreen tree (see Fig. 3-8).

■ **3-8** *A three-cone evergreen tree.*

Science skills

Observing, following directions, manipulating materials, creating a model

What you need

☐ Green construction paper
☐ Scissors
☐ Glue

To create a Christmas tree you will also need:

☐ White construction paper
☐ Markers
☐ Glitter
☐ A toothpick

Directions

1. Trace the three cone patterns in Figs. 3-9 and 3-10 onto green construction paper. Cut them out. These are half-circles.

2. To make a cone, place a half-circle on a flat surface in front of you with the flat edge at the top.

3. Curl Point A and Point C toward you until a cone lip forms at Point B.

4. Overlap points A and C, and glue the cone to make it hold its shape. Repeat until you have created three cones (Fig. 3-11).

5. Cut narrow fringes around the bottom of each cone. Curl the fringes up around a pencil. Stack them as shown in Fig. 3-12.

6. To turn the evergreen into a Christmas tree, trace the decorations in Fig. 3-13 onto white construction paper. Cut out four of each decoration. Color them with markers. Add glitter to the bell and the star. Draw a face on the gingerbread boy. Glue one star onto a toothpick and insert it in the top of the tree. Glue the other decorations all over the tree.

☞ Activity idea: Coloring summer and fall leaves

₽ Science skills
Recording information

The leaf pages are shown in Figs. 3-14 through 3-19. Duplicate each leaf page for each child. Staple them together with a cover sheet on top. Encourage the children to design a cover for their own Summer and Fall Leaf Book. The children will color the leaves as indicated on the pages to be copied.

Roots are underground branches of the tree. Roots help hold a tree in the ground and absorb water and nutritious minerals to help the tree grow. Trees have very big roots and tiny roots.

Most trees produce flowers and/or fruits. Some trees have beautiful flowers that we can see very easily, like a magnolia, yellow poplar, and dogwood. Some trees produce flowers that we can barely see so we never think about the flowers being there.

> ### *Pollen Point*
> *Some trees reproduce by means of spores.*

Fruits of trees are very different. Some trees have fruits that we can eat (like apples, cherries, peaches, and oranges). Many trees produce fruits that we do not eat, but some animals can eat them. The fruit of the tree has the important duty of protecting the seeds.

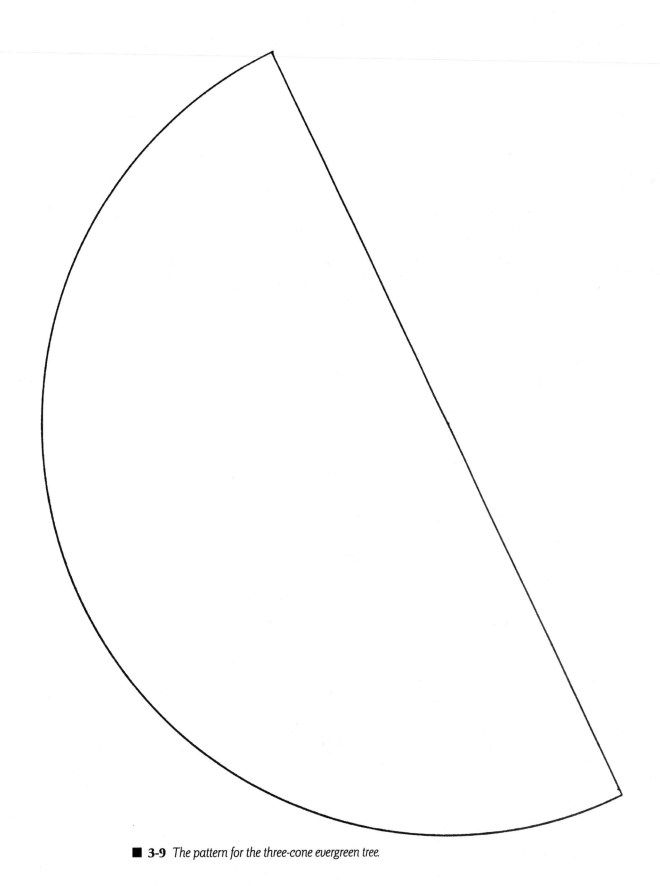

■ **3-9** *The pattern for the three-cone evergreen tree.*

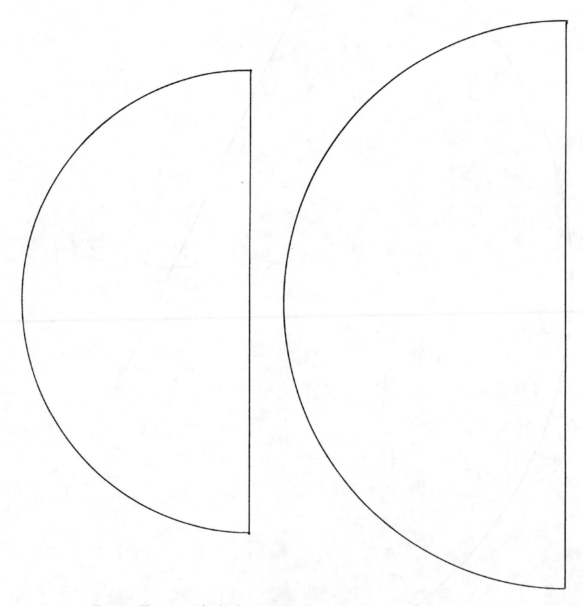

■ **3-10** *The patterns for the three-cone evergreen tree.*

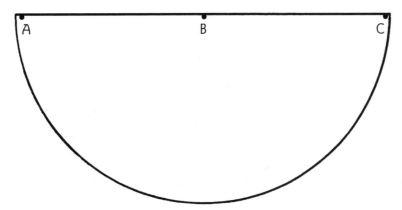

To make a cone, place a half-circle on a flat surface in front of you.

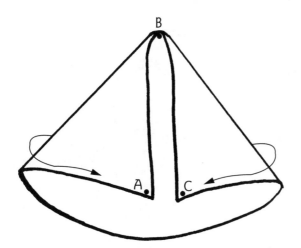

Curl point A and point C toward you until a cone tip forms at point B.

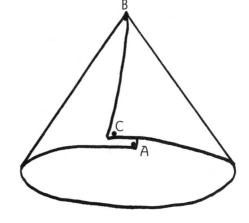

Overlap points A and C, and glue the cone to make it hold its shape.

■ **3-11** *How to overlap and glue the cones.*

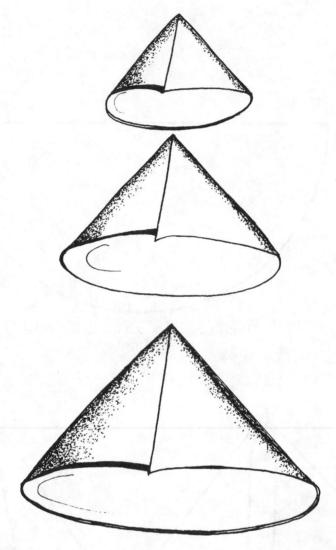

■ **3-12** *Stack the cones to make a tree.*

■ **3-13** *The patterns for the Christmas tree decorations.*

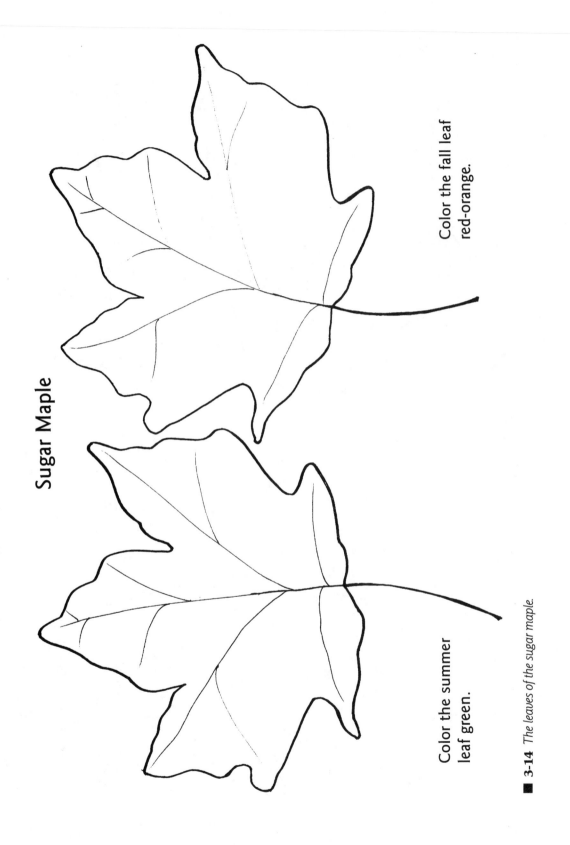

Sugar Maple

Color the fall leaf
red-orange.

Color the summer
leaf green.

■ **3-14** *The leaves of the sugar maple.*

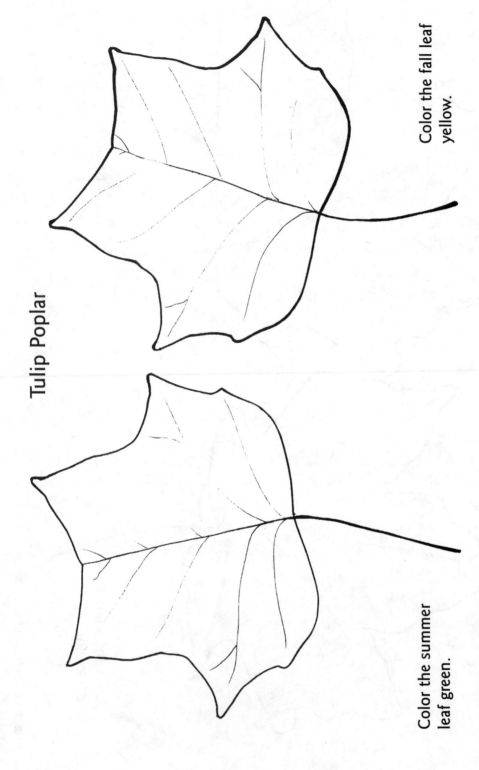

Color the fall leaf yellow.

Tulip Poplar

Color the summer leaf green.

■ **3-15** *The leaves of the tulip poplar.*

Post Oak

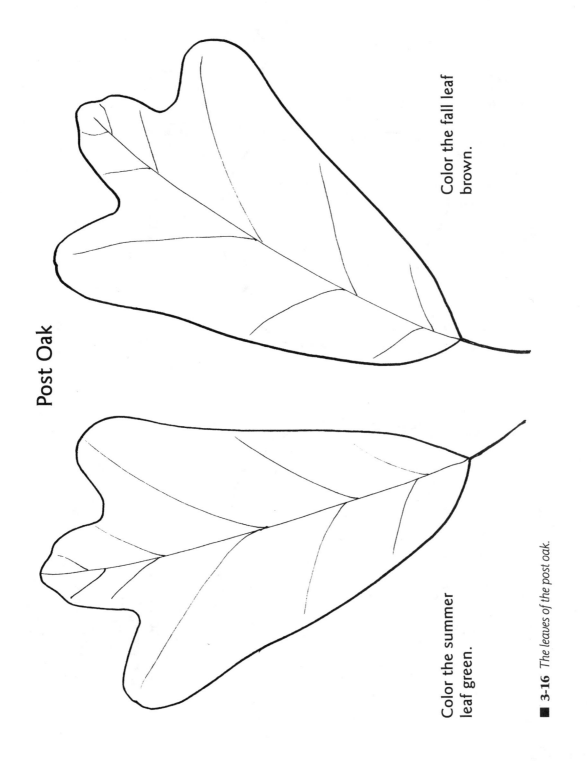

Color the fall leaf brown.

Color the summer leaf green.

■ **3-16** *The leaves of the post oak.*

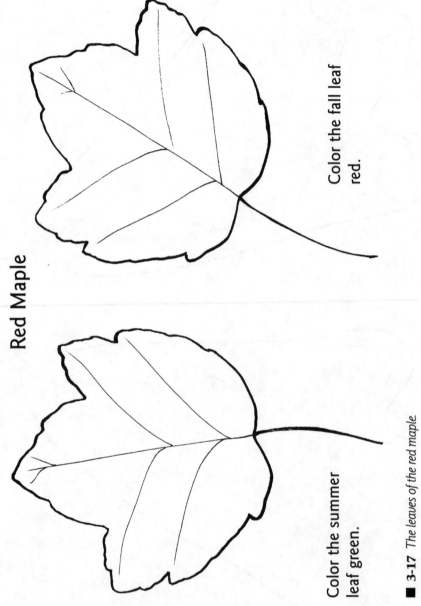

Red Maple

Color the fall leaf red.

Color the summer leaf green.

■ **3-17** *The leaves of the red maple.*

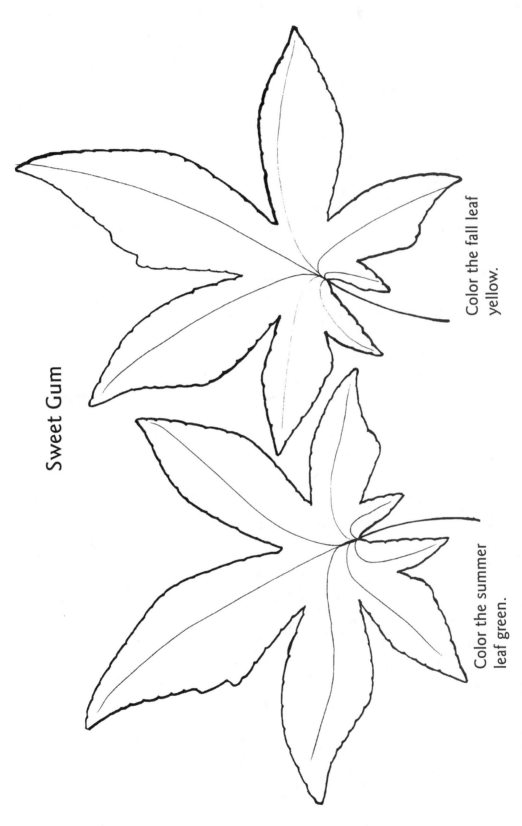

Sweet Gum

Color the fall leaf yellow.

Color the summer leaf green.

■ **3-18** *The leaves of the sweet gum.*

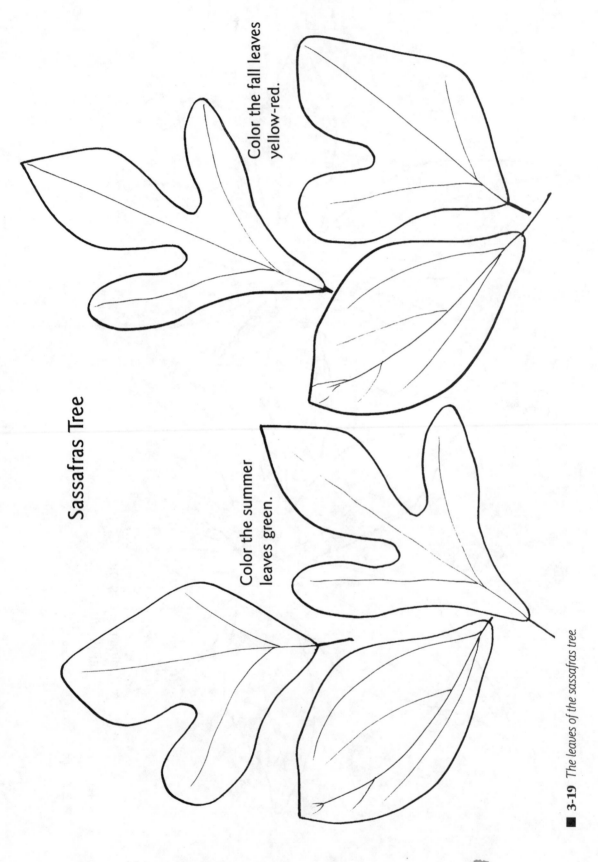

Sassafras Tree

Color the fall leaves yellow-red.

Color the summer leaves green.

■ **3-19** *The leaves of the sassafras tree.*

Activity idea: Apple Day

Science skills

Observing, classifying, measuring, using numbers, finding information, recording information

Plan a whole day (or several days) of Apple Activities. Send a note home several days ahead for every child to bring an apple. Encourage parents to look for an interesting type of apple to send. There are so many varieties in the grocery stores.

On the day that the children bring the apples, have a large basket available to put them in. Plan a time when you can take the apples out, one by one, to look at them and talk about them. In your discussions, talk about how each looks (color, shape, smoothness) and feels. Have a chart available (encyclopedias have good ones and many times grocery stores have charts also) so that you can identify each apple as a Red Delicious, Yellow Delicious, Granny Smith, etc. Categorize the apples and then count them. Which kind do you have more of?

Which color do you have more of?

For older students, provide a map of the United States. Show them some of the states where apples are grown: Washington, New York, Michigan, Pennsylvania, North Carolina, Virginia, West Virginia, and California. Apples are grown in other countries like Russia, France, China, and Germany. You might want to find these countries on a globe.

Use balance scales to see which of two apples is heavier. Another weighing activity is to put an apple on one side of the scale and then put other objects on the other side. For example, how many pennies does it take to equal the weight of this apple?

Give each child the apple he brought or provide one apple per child. Give each child a piece of white paper. Let each child draw and color his apple on the paper. The children can also write the name of the apple.

Plan a time for a tasting experience. Wash different kinds of apples. Cut them up into small pieces and let the children try several kinds. Talk about how each tastes. Make a graph to show what each child likes best. Save the seeds from the apples for the children to examine and count.

When the exploring is over, plan to make Applesauce. (The recipe can be found in the cookbook in this book.)

Throughout the day, you can sing this song to the tune of "The Farmer in the Dell."

Apples grow on trees.
Apples grow on trees.
I love apples,
Apples grow on trees.

Apples grow from seeds.
Apples grow from seeds.
I love apples,
Apples grow from seeds.

Apples can be red.
Apples can be red.
I love apples,
Apples can be red.

Apples can be green [or yellow, or speckled].
Apples can be green.
I love apples,
Apples can be green.

Apples are crunchy.
Apples are crunchy.
I love apples,
Apples are crunchy.

Apples are good for you.
Apples are good for you.
I love apples,
Apples are good for you.

We made applesauce.
We made applesauce.
We love apples,
We made applesauce.

Let the children help you make a list of foods that are made from apples like: applesauce, juice, pies, cereals, and apple butter.

Let's create fruit necklaces

Oranges, lemons, and apples contain interesting seeds. To make this project, eat the fruit, and use the seeds to create necklaces (see Fig. 3-20).

Science skills

Observing, following directions, creating models, manipulating materials, communicating and recording information, drawing conclusions

What you need

☐ Fresh orange, apple, and lemon
☐ **For adult use**: A sharp knife to cut the fruit open
☐ Orange, yellow, and red construction paper
☐ Scissors
☐ Glue
☐ Paper punch
☐ Orange, yellow, and red yarn

Directions

1. The adult should cut open the fruit and count the seeds inside. Lay the seeds aside while you create the paper necklaces.
2. Use construction paper and the patterns in Fig. 3-21 to trace and cut out a red apple, an orange orange, and a yellow lemon.
3. Punch a hole in the top of each figure. String yarn through the hole to make a necklace of each one.

■ **3-20** *Fruit necklaces.*

4. Glue the orange's seeds in the middle of the paper orange. How many seeds are there? Write the number on the back of the paper orange necklace. Lay it flat to dry.

5. Repeat this step with the lemon seeds and the apple seeds.

6. After the necklaces have dried compare the number of seeds in your apple with the number of seeds in your friends' apples. Are they the same or are they different?

7. Compare the number of seeds in the oranges and in the lemons. Which fruit has more seeds? Do you think that most fruits of one kind, for instance most lemons, have the same number of seeds?

Let's create a four-seasons apple tree
This apple tree can sit on your table and change with the seasons! (See Fig. 3-22.)

 ## Science skills
Following directions, creating a model, manipulating materials

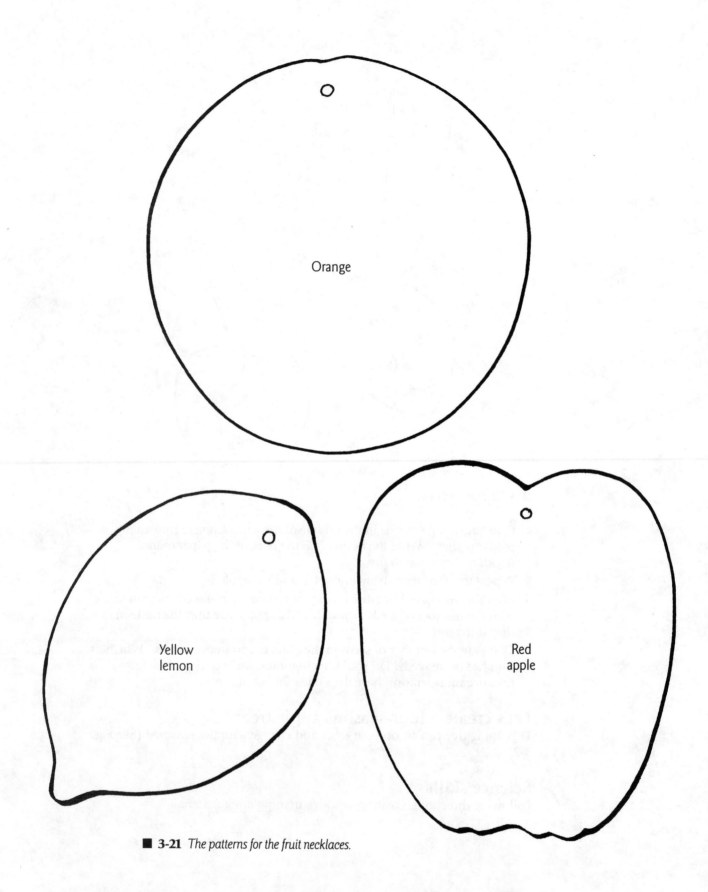

■ **3-21** *The patterns for the fruit necklaces.*

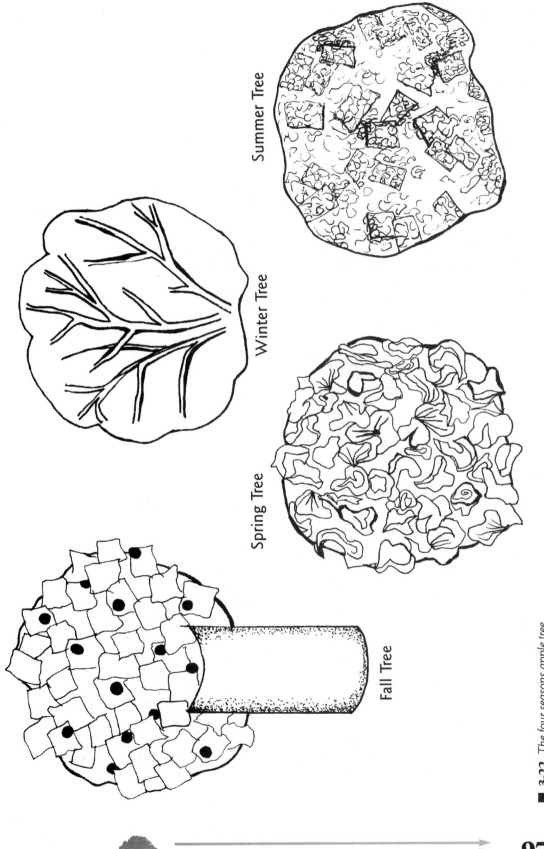

Summer Tree

Winter Tree

Spring Tree

Fall Tree

■ **3-22** *The four seasons apple tree.*

What you need

- ☐ One six-inch square of brown tissue paper
- ☐ Toilet paper roll cylinder
- ☐ Scissors
- ☐ Glue
- ☐ White poster paper
- ☐ Markers or crayons
- ☐ Green and pink tissue paper
- ☐ Red paper
- ☐ Paper punch
- ☐ Green and brown tempera paint
- ☐ Sponge
- ☐ Q-tip

Directions

1. Put a small amount of glue on the cylinder, and cover it with the brown tissue paper.
2. Tuck the paper into the cylinder at both ends. Cut two slits (1½ inches each) opposite each other on one end of the cylinder (Fig. 3-23).

■ **3-23** *Cut two slits in one end of the cylinder.*

3. Use the pattern in Fig. 3-24 to trace four shapes onto poster paper. Cut these out.
4. To create a flowering Spring Apple Tree, cut pink tissue paper into 2-inch squares. Press a square around the tip of your finger, forming a tiny cup. Dip the bottom of the cup into glue. Press it onto one tree shape so the

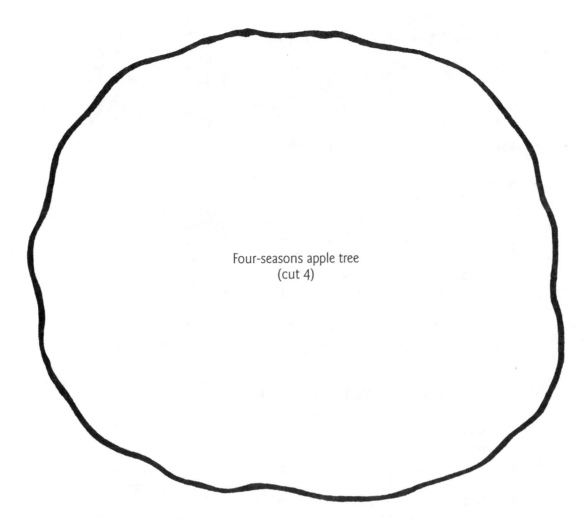

Four-seasons apple tree
(cut 4)

■ **3-24** *The pattern for the four seasons apple tree.*

tissue paper sticks up like a pink apple blossom. Repeat this step until the Spring Apple Tree is covered with blossoms.

5. To create a green Summer Apple Tree, dip the corner of a wet sponge in green paint. Gently dab a second tree shape with an up-and-down motion. The imprint of the sponge should be visible on the plate. This process of painting is called stippling.

6. To create a Fall Apple Tree, cut green tissue paper into 1-inch squares. Glue the squares all over a third tree shape. Add red apples to your tree by gluing on red circles made with a paper punch and red construction paper.

7. To create a Winter Apple Tree, Use a Q-tip to paint bare brown branches on the fourth tree shape.

8. After the glue and paint have dried on the tree shapes, you can insert them one-at-a-time in the tree trunk to show how an apple tree changes with the seasons.

> ## *Pollen Point: Peeling an apple*
>
> *If you start at the top and turn the apple as you peel, you can make one long curling piece of apple peel. In the olden days housewives were considered to be good cooks if the peels of their apples were very long. Contests were held to see which woman could create the longest single peel from an apple!*

 ## Discussion idea: Trees I know

 ## Science skill
Communicating information

Let the children tell about trees in their own yard. They may want to bring in pictures to show. Let them share any experiences they have had with trees, like having a treehouse, picking apples, or having a picnic under a tree.

We should be thankful for trees. Trees serve very important purposes in our lives. Trees make our world beautiful. Think of all the beautiful colors they provide for us to enjoy. They give us shade. Trees give us oxygen to breathe. Trees give us fruit and nuts to eat. Trees give us wood to build houses, furniture, and many things that we use every day. Trees provide homes for many animals.

 ## Activity idea: Let trees inspire you

 ## Science skills
Observing, recording information, applying knowledge

Plan a time to take the children outside to write a story, write sentences that share information, write a poem, or just draw pictures. They will need paper, pencils, and crayons (and/or water color paints). Let them sit under a tree or beside a tree or away so they can look at many trees. The point is that in order to write about trees, we need to be with trees, not in a classroom. Plan time on another day to come back outside for a sharing time when each child can share his writing with the other children.

Trees give us food to eat. Some of the foods that come from trees are: apples, pears, peaches, oranges, bananas, coconuts, walnuts, and pecans.

Trees provide wood for our homes, furniture, toys, and many other items we enjoy.

 ## Activity idea: Things that come from wood

 ## Science skills
Observing, classifying, asking questions, finding information, recording information

Let the children walk around the room to find things that are made of wood. Before the children start, talk to them about the differences between metal, plastic, and wood. Give them some examples of things made of each. After the children have finished walking around the room, let them all sit together.

You can make a list on chart paper, of the things in the room that are made of wood. Each child can tell one or two things and you can write these on the chart.

For homework, send a note home asking parents to help their children find things at home that are made of wood. Ask them to make a list and send it to school the next day. This will be a great assignment that parents and children can do together.

Trees provide medicines and products like latex that comes from a rubber tree in order to produce rubber.

We could not live without trees because trees produce oxygen which we need to breathe.

 ## Activity idea: Tree mural

 ### Science skills
Communicating information, applying knowledge

Plan a mural for the room or hallway. You will need blue paper for the background. You can make fantastic tree trunks by sponge painting onto light brown paper. Cut large trunks (with branches) out of light brown paper. Get a large rectangular sponge and cut it into four pieces. Get four different colors of paint for bark, like: gray, dark brown, light brown, and beige. Let the children use these colors to sponge paint bark on the trunks and branches. The effect will really be amazing.

The top of the tree (leaves) can be done in a similar way. Cut appropriate sized crowns for each tree out of a color of paper that you want the leaves to be. Cut the sponge into leaf shapes. For example, suppose you want to create a weeping willow tree. You could cut a large green circular shape from the paper. Then cut a slender leaf shape from a sponge. Have green paint available. The child will dip the sponge leaf into the paint and paint leaves all over the green top of the tree.

When the trunks and the crowns are finished, glue the trunk onto the crown and add each one to the blue background. Let the children add other things to the mural. They may want to put children, birds, their school, or whatever they think will make it wonderful.

Let children write thank you notes to trees, thanking them for the food they provide, the shade, the wood, and the oxygen. Add these written notes to the display.

Activity idea: Planting a tree

Science skills
Observing, following directions, manipulating materials, measuring, finding information, recording information, applying knowledge

Choose an area where the children can plant a young tree. You may want to get a seedling (1–2 feet tall) or a sapling (3–5 feet tall). In many ways a seedling is better because it will be easier to measure and observe. The children will need to help with the entire process (with adult guidance), from choosing the site to watering the planted tree.

After you have chosen a suitable place for your tree, decide on a type of tree that grows well in your area and would grow well in that location. Also, think about how big the tree will eventually be and will that continue to be a good place for the tree over the coming years. You may want to call your forestry service, to see if they will give you a tree. A parent might be willing to bring in a seedling from their own yard or land they own. You can also purchase one from a local nursery.

Have a camera available to make pictures of this special event. The children will need to have a journal to keep their information about their special tree. Decide on a type of journal that will be appropriate, and have the journals ready for the day of the planting. One great idea for the cover is to make a photograph of the little tree the day you plant it, and make a copy on your own copier of the picture for each child. Glue the copy onto construction paper and let the children think of a title—something like "Our Tree."

Before you plant the tree, let the children look at the roots of the tree. This will be their only opportunity to see the roots.

 An adult will need to dig a large hole with a shovel. The hole needs to be about twice as wide and twice as deep as the area the roots take up. After you have dug the hole, replace some of the soil, with whatever additive soil or nutrients the nursery recommends. Place the tree in the hole and add the remaining soil. You may need to put a stake beside the tree to hold it firmly in place. Water the tree. Label the tree in some way.

Let the children complete the first page in their journal. They should put the date, draw a picture of the tree, and write the name of the tree. They can write words or sentences also.

During the first year the tree will need to be watered regularly. Post a chart to show who should water the tree each week.

Each week, the children could write a journal entry about the tree. Some ideas for journal entries are:

1. Use numbers. How tall is the tree? How many branches does the tree have? How many leaves does the tree have?
2. Study the leaves. Draw a leaf. Be sure to draw the veins. Describe its shape. (Do not let children pick a leaf off of the tree. Encourage them to use their eyes to see and their fingers to gently feel.) What color are the leaves?
3. What is around the tree? (Other plants, objects, animals)
4. Study the trunk. Use a tape measure to measure the distance around the trunk. How many inches or centimeters? Feel the trunk. Is it rough or smooth? What color is it?
5. Observe the tree three times during the day. Record the time and indicate if the tree is in the sun or shade. Possible times might be: 9:00, 12:00, and 3:00.
6. Write a report about that type of tree. Use informational books.
7. Write a letter to the class as if it is being written by the tree. What would the tree tell you if it could?

8. Continue to make photographs of the tree and let the children put copies of these in their journals.

9. Help children record any information about anything that is done to the tree (like pruning, fertilizing) and anything that happens to the tree.

10. Talk about living and nonliving things. Help the children understand that this tree is living (is alive) because it uses food and water to live and grow. Make a chart to show living and nonliving things that are in the child's environment.

Activity idea: Adopting a tree

Science skills

Observing, following directions, classifying, manipulating materials, measuring, using numbers, asking questions, finding information, making predictions, communicating and recording information, applying knowledge

Choose an interesting tree that the children would like to adopt, that is, spend quality time with it in order to learn about it, enjoy it, and protect it. This should be a large tree, at least large enough that the children can sit under it and it will provide some shade.

You can create a special journal for the study of this tree also. The cover could include a copy of a photograph of the tree or any other creative idea you may have. Plain, white paper will be best for the pages of the journal.

The following are ideas for activities. Children should make a journal entry for each activity that they do. Every page should be dated also.

1. Observe the tree during each of the four seasons. Make photographs and let the children color pictures of the tree as it looks in each season. Collect leaves throughout the seasons. Press the leaves between newspaper and lay a heavy book on top for about a week. Lay the leaves on construction paper and laminate or cover with clear adhesive plastic. What happens to the leaves during each season? What changes occur during the seasons? What kinds of seeds does this tree have? What kind of flowers does this tree have?

2. Study the trunk of the tree. Make bark prints by laying a piece of paper on the bark and rubbing a crayon across the top of the paper. Feel of the bark. How does it feel? What color is it? Measure the circumference of the trunk. An easy way to do this is to use yarn to go around the trunk, then measure the length of the yarn.

3. Study the branches of the tree. Can you reach any of them?

4. Study the leaves of the tree. What shape are they? What color are they? What do the veins look like? What do the leaves look like during Fall, Winter, Spring, Summer? Do the leaves fall off in the fall? If the tree does lose its leaves in the fall, collect the leaves for study. Let the children make leaf rubbings.

5. Study the roots of the tree. Can you see any of the roots? What do they look like?

6. What plants or objects are around the tree? Are the other plants taller or shorter? Are there other trees like this one? Do you think someone

planted this tree or do you think it just came up by itself from a seed? Why or why not?

7. Are there any animals on the tree? (birds, ants, bees, squirrels, etc.) Are there any nests in the tree?

8. Look at the tree from a distance. Draw a picture of how it looks. Stand next to the tree and look straight at it. What do you see? Now lie down under the tree and look up into the tree. What do you see? Draw pictures and write words or sentences to answer these questions.

9. Take a bed sheet outside and lay it under the tree. Let the children lie on the sheet, on their stomachs with just their heads off the sheet. Ask them to look at the ground and see what is "under" this tree. They can use their fingers and magnifying glasses to explore the grass or dirt. Help the children record information in their journal.

10. Use informational books to write a report about this type of tree.

11. Put a blanket beneath the tree and let the children read books under its shade.

12. Let the children plan special games to play under their adopted tree.

13. Let the children plan special events to occur under or beside their adopted tree.

14. Write poetry about the tree.

15. Write stories about the tree.

16. Write letters as if the tree were doing the writing. What would the tree say?

17. Talk about ways you can help the tree? Does it need water? Do adults need to trim off branches? Does it need to be fertilized? Adults will need to help with these things, but it is important for children to understand that trees often need our help.

☞ Activity idea: Closure

Science skills

Observing, following directions, communicating information, applying knowledge

Review your initial goals and reflect upon what you have done throughout this study. Hopefully, the children are much more aware of the wonderful trees in their environment and they feel a sincere responsibility to care for them.

Here is a song that you and the children can sing about the tree you planted or your adopted tree. It can be sung to the tune of "Here We Go 'Round The Mulberry Bush," except this title will be "Here We Go 'Round The [tree type] Tree."

The children should join hands and form a circle around the tree. They should walk in a circle around the tree while they begin to sing the song. As they sing the verses, they should drop hands and pretend to do (or actually do) what the words say. Let the children decide on the words for the verses, but here are some suggestions:

Here we go round the _____ tree,
The _____ tree, the _____ tree.

Here we go round the _____ tree,
So early in the morning.

This is the way we feel the bark,
Feel the bark, feel the bark.
This is the way we feel the bark,
So early Sunday morning.

This is the way we hug the tree,
Hug the tree, hug the tree.
This is the way we hug the tree,
So early Monday morning.

This is the way we water the tree,
Water the tree, water the tree.
This is the way we water the tree,
So early Tuesday morning.

This is the way we sit in the shade,
Sit under the tree, sit in the shade.
This is the way we sit in the shade,
So early Wednesday morning.

This is the way we play in the leaves,
Play in the leaves, play in the leaves.
This is the way we play in the leaves,
So early Thursday morning.

This is the way we skip around,
Skip around, skip around,
This is the way we skip around,
So early Friday morning.

This is the way we rest by our tree,
Rest by our tree, rest by our tree.
This is the way we rest by our tree.
So early Saturday morning.

Let's create a pine-cone animal feeder
This feeder is not too messy. Squirrels love it, and so do bluejays, finches, chickadees, cardinals, and other birds.

Science skills
Following directions, manipulating materials, measuring

What you need
☐ A pine cone
☐ String
☐ Wax paper
☐ ¼ cup peanut butter
☐ ¼ cup bread crumbs (Make your own from bread scraps)
☐ 1 cup bird seed

Directions

1. Tie the string near the top of the pine cone so it can be hung. Lay the pine cone on wax paper.
2. Measure the peanut butter and bread crumbs into a bowl. Mix with a wooden spoon until smooth. Spread this mixture on the pine cone.
3. Roll the pine cone in bird seed, pressing on as many seeds as possible.
4. Hang the feeder on the Wildlife Tree.

Let's create a wildlife tree

Decorate the bare branches of a winter tree with treats for wild animals. (See Fig. 3-25.)

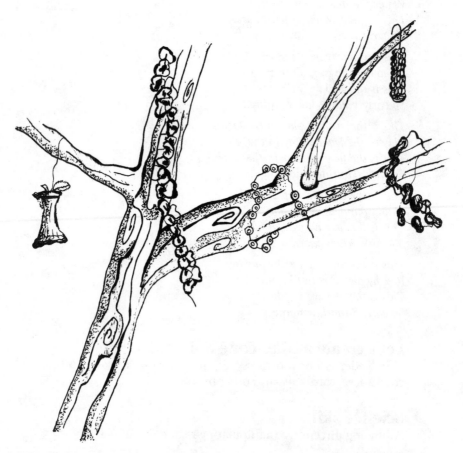

■ **3-25** *The wildlife tree.*

 ## Science skills

Observing, finding and recording information, asking questions, following directions, manipulating materials

What you need

☐ Information about birds and animals in your area
☐ A bare winter tree that you can watch some of the time

What kind of animals live near me?
Are there sparrows and pigeons and robins to see?
Pigeons like popcorn thrown on the ground.
Robins eat worms! Are there any to be found?
Will they fit on a string?
Oh, what will visit my Wildlife Tree?
What kind of animals live near me?
Squirrels and rabbits and foxes, maybe?
I'll hang carrots down low and corn up high.
Can I string some berries and make acorn pie?
How I hope that I can see
What will visit my Wildlife Tree!

By Joanna Vansant

☐ String

☐ Foods to hang on the tree, such as dried corn on the cob, Cheerios®, Pine Cone Feeder (directions follow), popcorn, peanuts in the shell, roasted chestnuts, cranberries, apple cores (eat the apples first).

Directions

1. Find out what animals live in your area. First observe animals that you can see, and make a list of them. Second, locate a naturalist or someone else who has a special interest in the wildlife around you, and ask them questions. Add new wildlife to your list.

2. Find out what kinds of foods each animal or bird eats. Record it on your list.

3. Select a tree that you can watch some of the time. Perhaps you can see it from a window during the day. This will be your Wildlife Tree.

4. Try to select foods that are as natural as possible, containing little or no sugar or salt. Figure out ways to hang each food on the tree by using string.

5. After the Wildlife Tree is decorated observe the animals that come to visit it, and record their names and what they choose to eat. Which treats disappeared first? Which ones were eaten last or were not eaten at all? Can you find out why?

The wildlife tree

Can you imagine doing without fresh crisp apple slices, orange juice, and lemonade? These things come from trees. Without trees we would also have to give up coconut cake, cherry pie, almond cookies, maple syrup, cinnamon toast, and root beer. Thank goodness for trees!

The Tree Cookbook

How to make Applesauce

1. Peel 20 apples
2. Cut them up
3. Add 1 c. sugar, 1/4 c. water, and cinnamon
4. Cook in crock pot
5. Cool and stir

By Elizabeth Dondiego

Make a fresh tree-tasting platter

Visit a grocery store and buy some fresh fruits that grow on trees. Cut them up and arrange them on a plate for sampling. Include apple slices, orange slices, plums, pears, peaches, cherries, prunes, and grapefruit.

Make homemade applesauce

Ask each child to bring an apple for the sauce. The adult peels and cuts; the children do the rest. This recipe uses a crock pot.

What you need

- ☐ 20 medium apples
- ☐ **For adult use**: A sharp knife to cut the apples
- ☐ 1 cup sugar
- ☐ 1 teaspoon cinnamon (One sift per apple)
- ☐ ¼ cup water

Directions

1. Start this recipe early in the day. Wash the apples. The adult should peel, quarter, and core the apples with the children sitting around her. Because the adult will need to use a knife, the children should sit three or four feet away for safety. The children should carry out the rest of the directions.
2. Put the apples in a crock pot. Measure and add the sugar.
3. Each person can sift a little bit of cinnamon onto the apples.
4. Add ¼ cup water. Cover the crock pot and cook on HIGH for one hour. Reduce the heat to LOW and cook the apples for two or three more hours. The aroma will be wonderful!
5. Turn off the crock pot and let it cool for one hour before eating.

Tree drinks

Visit a grocery store and buy several Tree Drinks, beverages made of fruits that come from trees. Two suggestions are apple juice, made from crushed apples, and prune juice, made by boiling dried plums. To make the following tree drink recipes, you will need a simple plastic juicer and a sieve to strain out seeds and pulp.

Fresh lemonade

Freshly squeezed lemons make the very best drink!

What you need

- ☐ 6 lemons
- ☐ 1 cup sugar
- ☐ 1 cup very hot water
- ☐ 7 cups ice water

Directions
1. Roll each lemon on the table top, pressing down on it until it is softened. This will make it easier to juice.
2. Wash the lemons. Cut them in half and juice them. Strain the juice and set it aside.
3. In a pitcher, mix the sugar and the very hot water. Stir to dissolve the sugar.
4. Add the ice water and the strained lemon juice. Serve.

Yield: 2 quarts lemonade

Fresh limeade
Follow the recipe for lemonade, except use lime juice instead of lemon juice.

Fresh orange juice
Freshly squeezed oranges are so sweet they don't need added sugar. Simply cut them, juice them, strain the juice, and enjoy!

Grapefruit juice
Grapefruit juice is delicious when it's fresh. Cut the grapefruit, juice them, and strain the juice. Pink grapefruit is sweeter than yellow grapefruit.

Tree cookies

Lemon bars
Lemon bars are tangy and delicious.

What you need
- [ ] 1 box vanilla wafers, crushed into crumbs
- [ ] ⅓ cup melted margarine
- [ ] 2 eggs
- [ ] 1 cup sugar
- [ ] ½ teaspoon baking powder
- [ ] ¼ teaspoon salt
- [ ] 2 teaspoons grated lemon peel
- [ ] 2 tablespoons fresh lemon juice

Directions
1. Preheat the oven to 350°F.
2. Mix together the vanilla wafer crumbs and margarine. Press this mixture in the bottom of a square baking pan, 8 × 8 × 2 inches, to make the crust.
3. Mix together the eggs, sugar, baking powder, salt, lemon peel, and lemon juice. Pour over the crust.
4. Bake about 30 minutes. Let them cool, and then cut them into little squares.

Yield: 24 cookies

Coconut cookies

Coconut makes a wonderful tree cookie.

What you need
- ☐ No-stick cooking spray
- ☐ 7 oz. flaked coconut
- ☐ ¾ cup sweetened condensed milk
- ☐ ¼ teaspoon almond extract
- ☐ 1 teaspoon vanilla

Directions
1. Preheat the oven to 325°F. Coat a cookie baking pan with no-stick spray.
2. Mix together the coconut, milk, and flavorings.
3. Drop by teaspoonfuls onto the baking pan.
4. Bake about 15 minutes, until the edges are light brown. Remove the cookies from the pan immediately or they will stick!

Tree pies

Cherry pie

Cherry pie has been an American treat since the days of the pioneers.

What you need
- ☐ Refrigerated pie crust for a 2-crust pie
- ☐ A can of cherry pie filling

Directions
1. Preheat the oven to 425°F.
2. Refrigerated pie crust is already rolled into a circle. Follow the directions on the package to fit it into a pie pan.
3. Pour in the cherry filling. Cover the pie with the second crust. Cut slits in the top crust.
4. Bake until the crust is golden brown and the juice begins to bubble up through the slits.
5. Serve warm, not hot.

French apple pie

This yummy pie only needs one crust.

What you need
- ☐ Refrigerated pie crust
- ☐ A can of apple pie filling
- ☐ 1 stick margarine
- ☐ ½ cup brown sugar
- ☐ 1 cup flour

Directions

1. Preheat the oven to 425°F.
2. Refrigerated pie crust is already rolled into a circle. Follow the directions on the package to fit it into a pie pan.
3. Pour in the apple filling.
4. Mix together the margarine, brown sugar, and flour until it's crumbly. Spoon on top of the pie.
5. Bake for 50 minutes, until the top is browned and bubbly.

Another tree dessert

Peach crisp
Hot, bubbly peach crisp is easy to make.

What you need
- ☐ 1 can (29 oz.) sliced peaches, drained
- ☐ ⅔ cup brown sugar
- ☐ ½ cup flour
- ☐ ½ cup oatmeal
- ☐ ¾ teaspoon cinnamon
- ☐ ¾ teaspoon nutmeg
- ☐ ⅓ cup margarine

Directions

1. Preheat the oven to 375°F. Grease a pan 8 × 8 × 2 inches.
2. Pour the peaches into the pan. Mix together the remaining ingredients and sprinkle over the peaches.
3. Bake 30 minutes until the top is golden. Serve warm.

Tree jelly
Visit a grocery store and buy several kinds of Tree Jelly, jellies, jams, and preserves made of fruits that come from trees. These might include apple jelly, orange marmalade, cherry preserves, and plum jam. Taste them on toast or soda crackers.

Nuts from trees
At the grocery store, look for nuts that come from trees. Buy some and bring them back to taste. Some to include are pecans, filberts, walnuts, and almonds. Look for almond cookies and pecan breakfast rolls, too.

Tree sap
Maple Syrup comes from the sap of a Sugar Maple tree and a Black Maple tree. The sap is collected in the early spring and is boiled to remove water and turn the sap into thick syrup. When all the water is removed, the sap is turned into wonderful tasting Maple Sugar Tree Candy.

Tree bark

Cinnamon is made of the inner bark of a cinnamon tree! Mix cinnamon with sugar, and sprinkle it on hot buttered toast for a terrific Tree Bark Treat.

Tree roots

The sassafras tree has a sweet smelling orange root. Wash the root, and then boil it in water. The water turns into fragrant sassafras tea. Add some sugar to it. It's delicious hot or cold. If you ever get to taste sassafras tea, you'll recognize the taste and aroma as that of root beer! Although root beer is now made with artificial flavoring, the original root beer was made from the root of the sassafras tree, hence its name. Root beer is a terrific Tree Drink!

Index

A

activities
  apples, 93-99
  apron, 21-22
  bookmark, 62-63
  bouquet, daffodil, 53-55
  bulletin board, 63
  cereal box book, 13-15
  coloring book, 47-50, 82-92
  cooking, impact on children, 22
    (see also recipes)
  crown, fall leaf, 76-78
  daisy, construction paper, 59-61
  evergreen, three-cone, 81-82
  feeder, 105-106
  field trips, 12, 42
  flower book, 63-64
  flower shop, 64-65
  flowers, observing and examining,
    43-44, 46
  fruit necklace, 94-95
  games, 17-19
  journals, 3, 42-43, 71
  leaf-print eggs, 80-81
  leaves in wax paper, 77-80
  mosaic, seed, 4-6
  murals, 64, 101
  nature walks, 44-45, 75-76
  pansy, coffee filter, 55-56
  peony, tissue paper, 51-53
  planting, 19, 101-103
  play, seed, 11-12
  poetry, 46
  seeds and water, 16-17
  seeds, locating and observing, 9-12,
    14-16
  songs, 93-94, 104-105
  sunflower, paper plate, 47-53
  tree-things picture, 71-72
  trees, adopting, 103-104
  trees, observing, 75-76, 100
  tulip, construction paper, 56-59
  walnut shell rabbit, 3-4
  wildlife tree, 106-108
  wood products, locating, 100-101

B

blade, 76

C

chlorophyll, 76

coloring book, trees, 82-92
cooking
  appliances in the classroom, 23-24,
  impact on children, 22
  rebus chart, 23
  recipes (see recipes)
cotyledons, 16
crown, 70

E

embryo, 16
evergreens, 76

F

field trips
  grocery store, 12
  nursery, 42
flowers
  activities (see activities)
  definition of, 42
  examining, 46
  parts of, 43-44
fruit, definition of, 2

G

games, 17-19
garden, flower, 45-46
grocery store field trip, 12

J

journal
  flower, 42-43
  seed, 3
  trees, 71

M

minerals, definition of, 70

N

nursery field trip, 42
nut, definition of, 2

O

ovary, 43

P

petals, 43
petiole, 76
photosynthesis, 44, 76
pistil, 9
planting seeds, 19

plants, definition of, 2, 42, 70
plays, 11-12, 20
poetry, 46
pollen, 9
pollination, 43

R

recipes
  applesauce, 110
  bark treat, 114
  bean soup, 36-37
  broccoli with cottage cheese dip,
    68
  candy, maple sugar tree, 113
  cauliflower with cheese, 68
  cherry pie, 112
  chili con carne, 37
  chocolate waffle iron cookies, 39-
    40
  cocoa bean, 39-40
  coconut cookies, 112
  cookies, 32-33, 36, 111-112
  corn, 26-30
  French apple pie, 112-113
  grapefruit juice, 111
  grits, 30
  hominy, 30
  hot chocolate, 39
  jelly, 113
  Johnny cakes, 27
  lemon bars, 111
  lemonade, 110-111
  limeade, 111
  macaroni, buttered, 34
  muffins, cornmeal, 28-29
  mush, fried cornmeal, 29-30
  nuts, 113
  oatmeal cookies, 32-33
  orange juice, 111
  pancakes, 33
  peach crisp, 113
  peanut butter, 35
  peanut butter cookies, 36-37
  peas, 38
  popcorn, 25
  popcorn balls, 25, 26-27
  rice, 31-32
  root beer, 114
  seed cookbook, 25-40
  soups, 36-38
  spaghetti, 34-35
  split pea soup, 38

Index

recipes *continued*
   tortilla chips with salsa, 29
   waffles, 32-33
   wheat, 33-35

S

scientific classification, 9
scientific method, 16
seed, definition of, 2
seed coat, 16
seeds
   activities involving (*see* activities)
   definition of, 9
   food source, 21

locating, 9-12
origin of, 9
parts of, 16
purpose of, 9
recipes (*see* recipes)
water experiment, 16-17
song, 93-94, 104-105
stamen, 9, 43
stem, 44
stigma, 43

T

trees
   activities involving (*see* activities)

adopting, 103-104
evergreens, 76
identification of, 76
leaves, parts of, 76
observing, 75-76, 100
parts of, 70
photosynthesis, 76
planting, 101-103
products of, 100-101
shelter, 72-75

V

vegetable, definition of, 2-3
veins, 76